BROADCASTING IN INDIA

Other volumes in this series include

Broadcasting in Sweden   **Edward W. Ploman**
Broadcasting in Canada   **E.S. Hallman** with **H. Hindley**
Broadcasting in Peninsular Malaysia   **Ronny Adhikarya** with **Woon Ai Leng, Wong Hock Seng** and **Khor Yoke Lim**
Broadcasting in the Netherlands   **Kees van der Haak** with **Joanna Spicer**
Broadcasting in Ireland   **Desmond Fisher**
Broadcasting in Guyana   **Ron Sanders**
Broadcasting in Japan   **Masami Ito** with **Hiroshi Shiono, Toshio Kataoka** and **Seigo Nagatake**
Broadcasting in Mexico   **Luis Antonio de Noriega** and **Frances Leach**

N.B. None of these books are available through Sage.

Case Studies on Broadcasting Systems

BROADCASTING IN INDIA

P.C. Chatterji

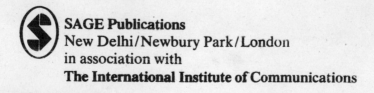

SAGE Publications
New Delhi/Newbury Park/London
in association with
The International Institute of Communications

First published in 1987 by

Sage Publications India Pvt Ltd
32 M-Block Market Greater Kailash - I
New Delhi 110 048

Sage Publications Inc  Sage Publications Ltd
2111 West Hillcrest Drive 28 Banner Street
Newbury Park, California 91320 London EC1Y 8QE

Published by Tejeshwar Singh for Sage Publications India Pvt Ltd, photo-typeset by Printers Plates and printed by Taj Press.

ISBN 0-8039-9529-6 (U.S.) 81-7036-046-3 (India)

To
my erstwhile colleagues in
Indian broadcasting

. . . I was again on a great voyage of discovery and the land of India and the people of India lay spread out before me. India with all her charm and infinite variety began to grow upon me more and more, and yet the more I saw of her, the more I realised how very difficult it was for me or for anyone else to grasp the ideas she had embodied. It was not her wide spaces that eluded me, or even her diversity, but some depth of soul I could not fathom, though I had occasional and tantalising glimpses of it. She was like some ancient palimpsest on which layer upon layer of thought and reverie had been inscribed, and yet no succeeding layer had completely hidden or erased what had been written previously.

Jawaharlal Nehru, *The Discovery of India.*

Contents

Foreword

In many different parts of the world official and unofficial enquiries, often protracted, are being carried out concerning the future of broadcasting. Some of them have recently been completed. In every case two points have almost immediately become clear. First, the future of broadcasting can never be completely separated from its past, even though the history of broadcasting in all countries is a recent one: there may be sharp breaks, not all of which are registered in legislation, but there are also continuities. Second, the future, like the past, will not depend on technological development alone. There are many exciting new communications technologies, many of them still in their early stages, but the speed and scope of their development will be determined by social, economic, political and cultural factors as well as by the technologies themselves. It has always been so.

Common technologies have been employed in different ways in different countries — sometimes with a few measures of control imposed by governments, by professional groups, or by trade unions, often with many. It is remarkable to what a great extent it is necessary to understand the general history of particular countries in order to understand what they have done with their conscious or unconscious communications policies.

This series of monographs, sponsored by the International Institute of Communications, is intended to direct attention to the main features of the communications patterns of a number of different countries. The studies deal with broadcasting structures rather than with the detailed processes of programme making or with the diffusion of news and ideas; and they seek first to explain how these structures came into existence, second, to identify what have been the landmarks in their histories, and, third, to elucidate what are the alternative possibilities envisaged for the future. Of course, a knowledge of the structures by itself is not enough to enable an adequate evaluation to be made of the quality of broadcasting output in any particular case. The same structure will generate different output at different times, and very similar structures will generate very different outputs.

Until recently it was thought possible to distinguish broadly between on the one hand system controlled by government and on the other hand systems linked with business through private enterprise and advertising. Yet there was always a third type of system, represented formidably by the BBC, which entailed neither government control nor business underpinning. This system, which was widely copied, was seldom copied in its entirety, and it now has many variants, most of which have deviated substantially from the model. In many countries there are now dual or multiple systems, in some cases, but not in all, subject to common 'supervision'; and in all countries there are degrees and nuances of control of broadcasting output whether by governments or by market forces.

The United States system, which is important not only in itself but because of the influence it has through exports of programmes and through diffusion of broadcasting styles, is itself a complex system — containing as it does a multiplicity of agencies and a changing public service element. It is hoped that United States experience will be covered in a later volume. There is increasing pressure there for a major review in the light of that experience and of continuing technological change affecting not only broadcasting but a wide and increasingly interrelated group of new communications technologies.

Alongside complex national structures, the products of time and place and in many cases deeply resistant to fundamental change, there are, of course, many few broadcasting structures in the world, including many which have come into existence in recent years in new countries. Many of these structures reveal themselves as extremely complex, too, when they are subjected to careful scrutiny. Nor are they necessarily very malleable. The more governments set out to chart and carry through conscious 'communications policies' — often related directly to their planning policies — the more they are compelled to consider the relationship of 'traditional' modes of communication to new technologies. The more, too, they are forced to establish priorities. This series includes, therefore, a number of countries where such policies have been formulated or are in the course of formulation.

Measuring the distance between policy formulation and policy implementation or effectiveness is, of course, at least as difficult in this field as in any other, and interesting work is being carried out by scholars in several countries on promise and performance. This series of studies, however, is less ambitious in intention. The studies are designed to provide accessible and reliable information rather than to evaluate the quality of achievement. The first cases chosen include some where there is no existing manageable monograph and some where the particular experience of that country is of general interest at the present time. The countries selected include some which are old and some which are new, some which are big and some which are small.

As the series unfolds, there will be increasing scope for comparison and contrast, and international patterns will doubtless be revealed — of 'models', of 'imports' and 'exports', of regional 'exchanges', and of relationships between different media. As such, comparison and contrast become more sophisticated than they have been in the past, any conclusions reached will be of increasing value in the future to those policy makers who are concerned to see their own circumstances in perspective and to frame their choices clearly.

Meanwhile, the International Institute of Communications, formerly called the International Broadcast Institute, which first launched this series, will continue to concern itself with the general opportunities and problems associated with the continuing advance of communications technology. The Institute is an international body which seeks to bring together engineers and social scientists, lawyers and programme-makers, academics and administrators.

The author of each case study in this series has been free to assemble and to present material relating to his own country in a manner decided upon by him, and he alone is responsible for the evidence offered and for the conclusions reached. Yet guidelines have been given to him about arrangement and coverage. Thus, he has been encouraged to ask questions as well as to compile facts. What have been the critical points in the history of broadcasting? How have that history and the broadcasting structures which have been evolved been related to the history of other forms of communication (the Press, for example)? What are the main institutional relationships at the present time? What are likely to be the future trends? Is it possible to talk of an integrated 'communications policy' in the case of the country under review?

The International Institute of Communications has no views of its own as an institution on the answers to such questions, but its Trustees and members believe that answers should be forthcoming if debate is to be both lively and well informed. Much of the serious study of cómmunications systems has hitherto been carried out within the confines, cultural as well as political, of national boundaries, and it is such research which most easily secures financial support. This series will point in a different direction. It is not only comparison and contrast which are necessary but a grasp of what problems and opportunities are common to countries, not necessarily alone but in the great continental broadcasting unions or other groupings between states.

We can now trace the beginnings of a 'global' sense in communications studies. Indeed, the word 'beginning' may be misleading. The sense certainly long preceded the use of satellites and was anticipated in much of the nineteenth century literature. The world was being pulled together; it was becoming a smaller place; everyone, everywhere, it was suggested, would be drawn in, instantaneously.

Communications policies, of course, have often failed to unite: instead, they have pulled people apart in clashes of images as well as in wars of words. And some of the case studies in this series will show how.

Two final points should be made. First, nothing stands still in communications history, and there are bound to be changes between the writing of these case studies and their publication. The processes of implementation of policy changes are often protracted. Second, it may well be that we are moving out of the age of 'mass broadcasting' as we have understood it into a new age of electronic communication. In that case, these studies will appear at a strategic time and will deserve careful study separately and together.

Asa Briggs
. *Worcester College, Oxford*

The National Environment for Broadcasting

1

Population

A t the 1981 Census the total population was 684,million. This figure, however, does not include the state of Assam where the Census could not be held due to various reasons. Taking this into account, the total population in 1981 is assessed at 700 million. In 1951, shortly after Partition, the population was 361 million, in 1961, 439 million, and in 1971, 548 million. The rate of growth of the population was 41.7 per thousand in the first decade referred to above, 41.12 in the second, and 36 in the last. Between 1961 and 1971 the death rate had, however, fallen from 27.4 to 18.92 per thousand. The death rate in 1981 was 14.8 per thousand. This speaks well of the country's health services but also indicates why the family planning programme has assumed growing importance for successive governments.

Of India's population, 80 per cent lives in the villages. Over the past two decades there has been a substantial movement of the population from the villages to the urban centres. One hundred and forty-eight towns have a population of one hundred thousand persons and nine of these have populations exceeding a million. The top four among these cities are:

| Calcutta | 9,165,650 | Delhi | 5,227,730 |
| Bombay | 8,202,759 | Madras | 4,276,635 |

Thereafter there is a sharp fall in population to three cities — Hyderabad, Ahmedabad and Bangalore with populations of approximately 2 million each — and then a further fall to several cities of just over one million persons apiece.

The average density of population for India as a whole worked out on the basis of the 1981 Census is 221 per square km. But there are enormous variations in the different geographical regions. For example, in the mountainous region in Himachal Pradesh the density is 76, in Sikkim it is 44, in Mizoram it is 23, and in Arunachal Pradesh, which borders China, Burma and Tibet, it is as low as 6. Some other fringe areas such as the Andaman and Nicobar Islands have a density of 23. In Rajasthan the average density is 100 and in the desert areas adjoining Pakistan, as in Jaisalmer, it may fall to 5. On the other hand, in Delhi state, population density reaches the record figure of 4,178 per sq.km.

India is well-known as a land of many religions. The percentages on the basis of the 1981 Census are:

Hindus	82.64
Muslims	11.35
Christians	2.43
Sikhs	1.96
Buddhists	0.71
Jains	0.48
Others	0.43

There are some 250 distinct tribes in India, constituting 7 per cent of the population.

Independence and Partition

Partition was a traumatic experience for the nation. While people were jubilant at the dawn of freedom and the new vistas which it seemed to herald, millions wept. Partition resulted in a gigantic two-way migration of Muslims to Pakistan and of Hindus and Sikhs to India and to brutal killings unprecedented in history. V.P. Menon, one of the top civil servants of the time, writing in his authoritative book, *The Transfer of Power in India*, (1957) estimates that up to the middle of 1948 approximately five and a half million non-Muslims were brought across the border from West Pakistan and approximately an equivalent number of Muslims moved from India to the other side. During the same period a million and a half Hindus crossed into West Bengal from East Pakistan, now Bangladesh.

At the same time there were widespread killings of Muslims, Hindus and Sikhs on both sides. These massacres enveloped Delhi,

Calcutta and certain areas of East Bengal. One of the most impressive events of these terrible times was the effort of Mahatma Gandhi to stop the carnage. In Calcutta, Gandhiji undertook a fast which was 'to end only if and when sanity returns to Calcutta'. The entire police force in Calcutta also fasted for a whole day while on duty, in support of the Mahatma. It took four days to work the miracle. Lord Mountbatten, in a broadcast, described Gandhiji as 'the one-man boundary force who kept the peace while a 50,000 strong force was swamped by riots'. A similar fast was undertaken in Delhi but eventually, on 30 January 1948, Gandhiji was murdered by a Hindu fanatic whilst addressing a prayer meeting in Delhi. The country mourned as never before.

While Partition posed an immediate problem of gigantic proportions, namely the rehabilitation of refugees, it also left in its trail the bitterness created by the two-nation theory. For the millions of Muslims who stayed behind in India, it has remained a problem to be accepted as they have sought to be and yet be integrated into the national life of the country. Despite free India's declared adherence to secularism, Hindu-Muslim riots and fears of discrimination against religious minorities, including Christians and others, have not disappeared.

The Constitution of India 1950

India gained her freedom on 15 August 1947, and the new Constitution declaring her a sovereign, socialist, democratic Republic came into operation on 26 of January 1950. The Constitution guarantees citizens 'Justice, social, economic and political; Liberty of thought, expression, belief, faith and worship; Equality of status and of opportunity'.

Part III of the Constitution sets out the Fundamental Rights of citizens which include equality before the law and equality of opportunity in matters of employment. It provides for freedom of speech and expression, the freedom to form associations and to assemble peacefully. 'Untouchability', or the practice whereby lower caste Hindus were treated as untouchable, is abolished. The right to acquire, hold and dispose of property is one of the fundamental rights. Several articles of the Constitution guarantee freedom of worship and the right to propagate religion. Discrimination on grounds of religion, race, caste, sex or place of birth is prohibited.

Part IV of the Constitution, which is described as the Directive Principles of State Policy, sets out certain principles of social justice which the state must endeavour to pursue. These include the right to an adequate means of livelihood, adjustment and control of material resources for the common good, equal pay for equal work for men and women, provision of free and compulsory education for children, and the promotion of the educational and economic interests of the scheduled castes, tribals and weaker sections of the community. While there is a common criminal law for all, certain matters such as marriage, divorce, inheritance etc are determined in accordance with the religious laws of the different communities. However, there is also a civil marriage act, which is open to all, and those married by it are governed by civil law. Article 44 lays down as a directive principle that 'the state shall endeavour to secure for all citizens a common civil code.' (Religious laws discriminate against women to a great extent). Article 51-A makes it a duty of every citizen of the state to 'foster scientific temper, a spirit of rational enquiry, humanism and reform.' The Directive Principles of State Policy, however, are not enforceable in a court of law.

The Indian union is a federal structure consisting of twenty-eight states and nine union territories. The distinction between states and union territories is mainly a carryover from the past, when certain areas were directly administered by the central government. Several Union Territories now have their own legislatures. Others, like Delhi and the Andaman and Nicobar Islands, function under a Lieutenant-Governor or Chief Commissioner who is directly responsible to the central government.

There is a division of functions between Parliament and the State Assemblies. Three separate lists of subjects are provided in the Constitution. A union list of subjects which fall within the jurisdiction of Parliament; a state list of subjects dealt with exclusively by state governments, and a short list of matters known as the concurrent list, which are the concern of both the central and state governments. Broadcasting, together with posts and telegraphs, telephones, wireless and other like forms of communication are in the union list and, therefore, are the exclusive responsibility of the union or central government.

The President is the head of the state and his position roughly corresponds to that of the Crown in the British system. The body responsible for governing the country at its apex is the Cabinet consisting of the Prime Minister and Council of Ministers. Each Minister, who is a duly elected member of Parliament, belonging to the majority party, is responsible for a Ministry which functions under him. The Minister is assisted by a Secretary to Government, who is the seniormost civil servant in his secretariat. The Ministry is the policy-making agency. Under the Ministry are Departments, as they are known, and these are the executive organisations.

Languages of India

The Constitution adopted in 1950 lays down that Hindi in the Devanagri script is the national language of India. It stipulated, however, that for a period of fifteen years English would continue to be used as the official language for all purposes of the Union, after which the matter would be reviewed by a committee. The official policy adopted after this period, and confirmed several times since, is that Hindi shall not be thrust on the non-Hindi speaking areas, until they themselves agree to accept it. Apart from English, fifteen languages have been specified as recognised languages: they include Sanskrit which, though hardly a spoken language today, is the mother of most Indian languages. The languages are Assamese, Bengali, Gujarati, Hindi, Kannada, Kashmiri, Malayalam, Marathi, Oriya, Punjabi, Sanskrit, Sindhi, Tamil, Telugu and Urdu. The Sahitya Akademi (the national academy for literature) annually gives awards to writers in the different languages and some languages other than the fifteen mentioned also figure in the list of these awards. Several minor languages or dialects have staked their claim to be recognised as full-fledged languages. Among these are Dogri, which is the language of the Jammu province of the state of Jammu & Kashmir, Konkani, a language of a substantial section of the people of Goa and Karnataka, and Nepali and Tibetan, the main languages of the Darjeeling district of West Bengal and Sikkim. Language is an important political and cultural issue in India with far-reaching implications for the national life of the country.

It has been said that no civilisation anywhere in the world with the probable exception of China, has been as continuous as that of India and language is an important root which nourishes the myriad flowers of civilisation. Sir George Grierson, the leading authority on the languages of India, states that there are no less than one hundred and seventy-nine languages and five hundred and forty-four dialects in the country. Grierson's distinction between what he calls minor languages, which do not have a written script, and dialects, is not very clear. In common usage, however, Indian languages fall into four main groups—the Aryan, the Dravidian, the Tibeto-Burman and the Austro-Asiatic. Of these four groups, the Tibeto-Burman and the Austro-Asiatic may be described as minor or as dialects, and between them account for approximately one hundred and twenty languages. The people speaking these languages constitute something like one per cent of the total population and are mainly tribal people inhabiting the hilly north-east corner of India. None of the Tibeto-Burman languages are included in the fifteen languages listed in the Constitution.

Of the listed languages Hindi, Urdu, Kashmiri, Sindhi and Punjabi constitute the northern group of the Aryan family, Assamese, Bengali and Oriya the eastern group, and Gujarati and Marathi the western group. The Dravidian family is represented by Telugu, Tamil, Malayalam and Kannada. The Aryan and Dravidian languages each have developed literary traditions which go back some three thousand years and the two have acted and reacted upon each other. The modern phase in these languages may be said to start from about AD 1200 to 1500. Among the northern group of Aryan languages the two most prominent are Hindi and Urdu. While they have a single basic structure and syntax, in its more literary forms Hindi harks back to Sanskrit while Urdu has its roots in Persian and Arabic. It emerged in the seventeenth century as a mixture of basic Hindi with words derived from Persian and Arabic which were brought to India by successive Muslim conquerors. For this reason, Muslim sentiment and cultural links centre on the preservation and development of Urdu, though Hindus too have made significant contributions to its literature and it is the mother tongue of many. Urdu is also the national language of Pakistan. With regard to Hindi or 'khari boli' (standard language) it should be pointed out that it has developed out of several dialects, such as Braj, Bhojpuri, Maithili, Maghadi and Avadhi which have ancient literary traditions and are the spoken language of millions. If they have lost ground to Hindi in the last two hundred years, each nevertheless commands powerful votaries who are constantly staking the claims of these languages to wider recognition.

Of the eastern Aryan languages, Bengali-speaking people constitute the largest group. Bengali has also been the language of powerful writers, one of whom, Rabindranath Tagore, was awarded the Nobel Prize for Literature in 1913. The Bengali language and literature have also exercised considerable influence over the other languages of the eastern group, Assamese and Oriya, and in literary matters, over Hindi and several other Indian languages. Of the western group the two main languages are Gujarati and Marathi, though Gujarati has close links with the languages of the north. Both have highly developed literatures.

The Dravidian languages fall into several groups. Telugu of the northern group, together with Tamil, Kannada and Malayalam of the southern, forms the most important of this language family in the country. Telugu is numerically the most important, and it has a very rich literary tradition. It has been considerably influenced by the Aryan languages. On the other hand, Tamil has preserved many old roots and words of primitive Dravidian and has retained certain literary forms which have no counterparts in the literature of the Aryan languages. Malayalam had its origin in old Tamil and became established as a separate language some time after the tenth century. It claims a continuous literary tradition from the fifteenth century. Kannada literature is said to have arisen in the middle of the first millenium. Jain writers have made notable contributions to its literature.

To appreciate the political significance of language we must take note of the development of British administration in India. At the time of Independence India consisted of two distinct parts — what was known as British India, made up of a number of provinces directly governed under the British Crown; and the Indian states ruled by the princes or Indian rulers owing suzerainty to the British Crown and guided in their internal affairs by a British Resident or Political Agent. This division itself was an accident following what was described by British historians as the Indian Mutiny of 1857 and is now known as the first war of Indian Independence. After 1857 there was no further annexation of Indian territories by the British. While those areas already directly administered by Britain became known as British India the others continued under their respective rulers. The boundaries of British Indian provinces were the result of convenience and accident. When the British advanced and occupied new areas, these were incorporated within the jurisdiction of the Governor of the adjacent province. When a territory became too large for efficient control by a single administration, it was split up into two or three provinces. And so this process went on. In 1918 the Commission of Indian Constitutional Reforms observed, 'We are impressed with the artificial and often inconvenient character of existing administrative units.' The Indian National Congress in its session in 1920 officially endorsed the view that linguistic provinces were desirable and a committee set up by the All Parties' Conference in 1928 under Pandit Motilal Nehru (Jawaharlal's father) lent its powerful support to the linguistic principle. It said, 'If a province has to educate itself and do its daily work through the medium of its own language, it must necessarily be a linguistic area... Language as a rule corresponds with a special variety of culture, of traditions and literature. In a linguistic area all these factors will help in the general progress of the province.'

In 1930 the Indian Statutory Commission, which considered the redistribution of the provinces, remarked that 'If those who speak the same language form a compact and self-contained area, so situated and endowed as to be able to support its existence as a separate province, there is no doubt that the use of a common speech is a strong and natural basis for provincial individuality.'

When the Congress Party came to power in 1947 it realised that while language might assist in the progress of a province or state, it could also become a threat to the unity of India. Nevertheless it was impossible for the party to repudiate completely the principle of state reorganisation on a linguistic basis. The government, therefore, set up in 1953 the States' Reorganisation Commission which submitted its report in September 1955. On the central issue, the Commission said, 'It is neither possible nor desirable to reorganise states on the basis of a single test of either language or culture, a balanced approach which takes all relevant factors into account is necessary.' It emphasised the importance of national unity and opined that in strategic areas, the administrative set up should be determined primarily by considerations of national security. In this context it favoured larger states in border areas, if they were not under the direct control of the centre.

Despite these weighty arguments the Government of India has found it impossible to resist the demands for states on a linguistic and cultural basis. Agitations have led to concessions. For example, Assam in the north-east corner of India—which the commission recommended, on grounds of national security and economic interdependence, should remain a single state — now consists of no less than five separate administrative units. The same thing happened in the state of Punjab which borders Pakistan. Cultural-linguistic separation remains a volatile force which has yet to find an appropriate place within the national consciousness.

The Economy

The Indian economy is predominantly agricultural. About half of the country's income is derived from agriculture and allied activities which provide employment for some three-fourths of its labour force. Much of the labour on the land is underemployed, particularly in certain seasons. The objective of centralised planning since 1951 has been to attain self-sufficiency in food, to expand and diversify industry and thereby to achieve all-round progress. Since, in the Indian conception, mass media are geared to the developmental effort, it is relevant to mention, very briefly, some of the major strategies in the agricultural and industrial sectors.

To free agriculture from dependence on the monsoon and other seasonal rains, major and minor irrigation projects in the shape of canals, dams, reservoirs, lift irrigation and other schemes have been undertaken. Increasing the acreage under cultivation, placing a ceiling on holdings, distributions of land to the tiller, improving inputs such as high-yielding varieties, fertilisers and improving storage and marketing facilities have been other major objectives.

India's industrial policy is guided by the fact that it is a mixed economy. There are three categories of products — those which are produced solely by government enterprises; those which are produced both in the public and private sector; and those which are entirely in the hands of private enterprise. Since Independence, the chief plank in the Government's policy has been the rapid and enormous growth of the public sector within the framework of national plans.

While in 1951 there were only five such undertakings with an investment of 290 millions, by 1983 the number had shot up to 209 with an investment of over 300.4 thousand million rupees. Public sector enterprises produce such diverse products as arms and defence equipment, aircraft, atomic energy, plant machinery, steel, coal, aluminium, copper, heavy and light engineering products, petroleum products, locomotives, ships, telephones and telephone cables, telegraph and wireless apparatus. Important minerals fall within the exclusive sphere of the public sector. In the sphere of joint operations come minerals, other than those confined to the public sector, machine tools, ferrous alloys, drugs, antibiotics, fertilisers, plastics and synthetic rubber.

So far as the private sector is concerned, the government follows a licencing system to ensure that monopolies do not establish a disproportionate hold on industry. A list of some nineteen items has been drawn up which are open to large industrial houses (the extent of foreign capital to be used is restricted). These include items such as metallurgical industries, ferro-alloys, steel castings and forgings, non-ferrous metals and their alloys, industrial turbines, internal combustion engines and electronic equipment.

In other areas the government gives preference to small and medium entrepreneurs. A number of development banking institutions have been set up to support private investment in industry. Considerable attention has been paid to import substitution and the development of indigenous technology. This policy has been largely successful and today almost everything from a pin to giant machinery, excluding a few highly sophisticated types of defence equipment, is being manufactured in the country.

The working population of India is about one-third of the total population. Of this work force, approximately 75 per cent is made up of cultivators and agricultural workers. These persons are described as the traditional workers or the non-organised sector of the work force. The organised sector comprises factory workers, who form by far the largest proportion, persons working in mines and quarries, trade and commerce, construction, transport, storage and communication and the like. Reliable data is available only in respect of workers in the organised sector of the economy, who constitute approximately 10 per cent of the labour force.

A number of measures have been introduced since independence to regulate working conditions, to provide for minimum wages, insurance, procedures for settlement of industrial disputes, workers' participation in management and the like. According to the latest figures, there are over 6,000 registered trade unions in the country. While the bargaining power of the unions is quite considerable in the organised sector, the government recognises that there is a good deal of exploitation among rural workers. For example, bonded labour was abolished by an Act of Parliament in 1976. Nevertheless, the Planning Commission in its Sixth Plan Document (1981) has accepted estimates of existing bonded labour as one hundred and fifty thousand and they are prepared to concede that the number may be twice as large.

Non-controversial data on economic levels and distribution of wealth are not readily available. Poverty estimates given by distinguished economists go back to 1960-61. Since the criteria for defining poverty are not uniform, the estimates given by different authorities are not comparable. Thus Dr B.S. Minhas, who was himself a member of the Planning Commission and resigned just before the finalisation of the Fifth Plan, in his book, *Planning and the Poor* (1974), estimates that, in 1960-61, 46 per cent of the urban population and 59.4 per cent of the rural population were below the poverty line. In 1967-69, his figures respectively for urban and rural populations were 37 per cent and 50.6 per cent. Another estimate for the year 1960-61, given by Dandekar and Rath in their work *Poverty in India* (1971) is that 38 per cent of the rural population and 48.6 per cent of the urban population live below the poverty line. M.S. Ahluwalia, in a paper *Rural Poverty in India* (mimeo), issued by the World Bank (1978) estimates that in 1960-61, 42 per cent of the rural population were below the poverty line.

The Planning Commission in its Sixth Plan Document (1981) stated that those below the poverty line in 1972-73 were '54 per cent in the rural areas and 41 per cent in the urban areas. The corresponding figures for 1977-1978 are 51 per cent and 38 per cent.' (page 28).

The estimates by Minhas and Dandekar and Rath given above do not even agree as to where the greater degree of poverty lies — in the rural areas according to Minhas, in the urban areas according to Dandekar and Rath. However, in this matter, Minhas' estimates follow broadly the same pattern as those of the Planning Commission. The Planning Commission, commenting on poverty, noted that 'various analyses of the movement of poverty percentages over a longer time period do not show a significant upward or downward trend. The broad picture is that of an increase up to the mid-sixties, when consumption standards were badly affected by two severe droughts, and a decline thereafter.' (page 29). Incidentally poverty is reckoned on the basis of a single criterion, calorie intake. Other essentials such as housing, clothing, education and elementary health care are not taken into consideration.

Literacy and Education

According to the Constitution, education is on the concurrent list of subjects, that is, it is within the jurisdiction of both the states and the centre. In practice, however, it is the states which deal with the important aspects of education such as determining the number of years of schooling, the medium of instruction, and curricula at all levels. The central government comes in to provide support in the form of advice on educational development and with funds for implementing development schemes. The centre endeavours to co-ordinate educational facilities, to determine standards of higher education, to provide assistance for scientific and technical education and research, and to promote the national language (Hindi) and other languages. The centre is responsible for running seven universities (known as Central Universities), five technical institutes (known as Indian Institutes of Technology), a chain of National Laboratories and several other institutes devoted to higher learning. The University Grants Commission, an autonomous body, was set up at the centre in 1953 to co-ordinate university education and to determine and maintain standards of teaching, examination and research in the universities. If we remember the respective roles of the centre and the states, many of the incongruities in Indian education can be better understood.

According to the 1981 Census, 36.17 per cent of the population are literate. In 1951, the figure was 16.6 per cent, in 1961, 24 per cent and in 1971, 29.4 per cent. Literacy for men is 46.74 per cent and for women 24.88 per cent. Rural folk and women seem to form the bulk of illiterates: the percentage of literacy is twice as high in urban areas as it is in the villages. According to the Directive Principles of the Constitution the state is to provide free compulsory primary education between the ages of six and fourteen years for all children. What has been achieved so far is free education in all states for children between the ages of six and eleven and it is compulsory in most states. Eighty-six per cent of children of this age group are actually in school today.

The fourth All-India Educational Survey published in 1980 by the National Council of Educational Research and Training, gives some basic information about school education. There were 475 thousand primary schools in the country. Of these, over 90 per cent were located in the rural areas and the vast majority were run by government. Of primary schools, 34.75 per cent are single-teacher schools and only 8 per cent of primary schools have more than five teachers apiece. The number of middle schools is put at 112 thousand, approximately 84 per cent of which are in the rural areas. In this case government is responsible for running 40 per cent of the schools, the remaining being run by local bodies and private groups. There were 36 thousand secondary schools and approximately 10,500 higher secondary schools. Of these 72 per cent and 43 per cent respectively are in the rural areas. Over 60 per cent of these schools are run by private bodies.

Over the five years ending in 1978, the enrolment in primary schools went up by 6.93 per cent, in middle schools by 10.13 per cent, and by 14.30 per cent at the secondary and higher secondary levels.

Because of the poor opportunities for employment a very large number of youngsters find that on leaving school they are not qualified for a job. Inevitably there is a tremendous rush for admission to colleges. In the last two decades the number of students in Indian universities has gone up nine times with dire effect on the standard of education. There are no less than one hundred and six universities in the country and ten institutions deemed to be universities.

Over the past three decades a big effort has been made to provide vocational training and technical education at polytechnics and other such institutions where practical training is provided. The Sixth Plan Document estimates that between 1950-51 and 1975-76 the number of students in engineering technological colleges increased from 13 thousand to 286 thousand. This picture of expansion holds true for other categories such as scientists, doctors and agricultural graduates. As the Planning Commission concludes, India now has the third largest scientific and technical work force in the world.

The problems of education in India are indeed complex and numerous. To begin with there is poverty, especially in the villages. From a very young age children start helping their parents in tending cattle, in the fields and in doing other odd jobs. So even if education is free, spending several hours at school means that the parents lose the labour which the child would have provided. The Planning Commission has estimated that at the primary and middle levels, for every three children going to school, one child is left out. What is more distressing is the huge drop-out rate in the first five years which the Commission puts at 64 per cent.

government. Of primary schools, 34.75 per cent are single-teacher schools and only 8 per cent of primary schools have more than five teachers apiece. The number of middle schools is put at 112 thousand, approximately 84 per cent of which are in the rural areas. In this case government is responsible for running 40 per cent of the schools, the remaining being run by local bodies and private groups. There were 36 thousand secondary schools and approximately 10,500 higher secondary schools. Of these 72 per cent and 43 per cent respectively are in the rural areas. Over 60 per cent of these schools are run by private bodies.

Over the five years ended 1978, the enrolment in primary schools went up by 6.93 per cent, in middle school by 10.13 per cent, and by 14.30 per cent at the secondary and higher secondary level.

Because of the poor opportunities for employment a very large number of youngsters find that on leaving school they are not qualified for a job. Inevitably there is a tremendous rush for admission to colleges. In the last two decades the number of students in Indian universities has gone up nine times with dire effect on the standard of education. There are no less than one hundred and six universities in the country and ten institutions deemed to be universities.

Over the past three decades a big effort has been made to provide vocational training and technical education at polytechnics and other such institutions where practical training is provided. The Sixth Plan Document estimates that between 1950-51 and 1975-76 the number of students in engineering technological colleges increased from 13 thousand to 286 thousand. This picture of expansion holds true for other categories such as scientists, doctors and agricultural graduates. As the Planning Commission concludes, India now has the third largest scientific and technical work force in the world.

The problems of education in India are indeed complex and numerous. To begin with there is poverty, especially in the villages. From a very young age children start helping their parents in tending cattle, in the fields and in doing other odd jobs. So even if education is free, spending several hours at school means that the parents lose the labour which the child would have provided. The Planning Commission has estimated that at the primary and middle levels, for every three children going to school, one child is left out. What is more distressing is the huge drop-out rate in the first five years which the Commission puts at 64 per cent.

Communications

A modern communications system has been in operation in India since 1854 when the Postal Department was set up. The most important carrier of mail is the Indian railways system which is the largest in Asia and the fourth largest in the world. Before the setting up of the railways, mail was carried on very few main routes and costs were high. The first railway line was opened in 1853, from Bombay to Thana, an important suburb today, covering a distance of just twenty-one miles. Travelling post offices started in 1870 and from 1907 the Railway Mail Service has functioned on a regular basis carrying letters and parcels throughout the country.

Between 1951 and 1977 post offices have trebled in number, telegraph offices have doubled and telephones have registered an eleven-fold increase. Trunk-dialling services now operate in 296 cities. Telex services are available between 172 cities within the country and between them have an installed capacity of 21,800 telex connections. India manufactures its own teleprinters and telephones. The microwave equipment for the second international satellite earth station set up in Dehra Dun was entirely designed and manufactured in the country.

India's external telecommunications services are operated by the Overseas Communications Service which has its headquarters in Bombay. It operates out of the country from four centres at Bombay, Calcutta, Madras and Delhi. It provides overseas telegraph, telephone, telex, radio-photo and leased telegraph channel services. It also arranges broadcast transmission and reception facilities for government news agencies and voicecasts for correspondents.

Microwave and telephone circuits for broadcasting purposes are provided by the Posts and Telegraphs Department on a rental basis. The anticipated demands of broadcasting are forwarded to this department which takes responsibility for providing circuits and meets the costs.

The electronics industry, which has made great strides since Independence, is spread over both the public and private sectors. A total ban on the import of radio sets and parts was imposed by the government in the early fifties and some twenty large scale units and several hundred small units are now producing approximately five million sets annually. Except for tubes which are still imported, TV sets, including colour sets, are being manufactured domestically.

Medium-wave transmitters of low to high power are produced in India as are radar, sonar, and navigational aids, and hard-as well as software for computers.

An Electronics Commission has been set up by the government to lay down policy guidelines for the healthy growth of the industry. A Department of Electronics is responsible for executive action. To ensure the balanced growth of the industry in different parts of the country, the Electronics Commission has provided assistance to State governments to set up corporations to manufacture equipment of various kinds.

India's first satellite earth station was commissioned in 1971. It is located at Pune and operates with the Intelsat satellite positioned over the Indian Ocean. The second satellite earth station started functioning in Dehra Dun in December 1976. Since then no less than twenty-eight additional earth stations have been set up in different parts of the country. There has been an increasing use of the Intelsat system by India since 1971. The minimum percentage of contribution for membership of Intelsat is 0.5 per cent: India's contribution today stands at 1 per cent, twenty-third among the contributors. For comparison, it is interesting to note the contribution of Malaysia at 0.86 per cent, Indonesia at 0.75 per cent and Thailand at 0.55 per cent.

The Indian Space Research Organisation (ISRO) is the research and development organisation of the Government of India's Department of Space. ISRO was responsible for the ground segment in the Satellite Instructional Television Experiment (SITE) conducted under an agreement with NASA for direct TV reception in 1975-76. All the equipment for this segment was manufactured in India. The software component was provided by AIR. Following the SITE experiment, under an agreement between ISRO and the Franco-West German enterprise the 'Symphonie' satellite was made available for two years from 1st June 1977 for telecommunication experiments. This experiment was designed as a system test of a geo-synchronous communications satellite and to improve Indian expertise in the design, development and operation of a communication system operating a geo-stationary satellite.

India's first multi-purpose domestic satellite was launched with US assistance on the 10 April 1982. It was designed to provide meteorological data, communication channels and telecasting facilities. The satellite had problems from the start as a result of which launching had to be postponed on two occasions. After corrective action the satellite was placed in its geo-stationary orbit on 20 April and started transmitting signals three days later. After being in orbit for 150 days it finally folded up on 4 September. India's second domestic satellite INSAT IB was successfully launched on 15 October 1983. Its use by Doordarshan to provide a network service and by AIR for news and other relays is discussed later in this book.

The Press

The Press in India celebrated its bi-centenary in 1980. It would be true to say that the importance which Indians attach to the freedom of the press stems from the fact that it was born in opposition to authority. Hickey's *Bengal Gazette*, which made its appearance in January 1780, had for its main target Warren Hastings who was Governor-General. While Hickey's venture closed down within the year, another journal called the *Indian Gazette* designed to project the viewpoint of the authorities had meanwhile come into existence. The Bengal example was soon followed in Madras and Bombay. The early newspapers, which were weeklies confined to a few pages, were all British-owned and it was not till 1816 that the first Indian-owned paper in English, also designated the *Bengal Gazette*, made its appearance. The first paper in an Indian language *Samband Kaumudi* was published around 1820 in Bengali under the editorship of the great social reformer Raja Ram Mohan Roy (1772-1833). *Vidanta Martand*, the first Hindi newspaper, a weekly, appeared in Calcutta in 1826. By 1833 there were over a dozen newspapers in Bengali and by mid-century there were also half a dozen each in Marathi and Gujarati. At this stage it was Raja Ram Mohan Roy who was the most progressive influence on the development and freedom of the Press, as he was on religious and social reform and in education. The first regular Hindi daily newspaper to come into existence was *Samachar-Sudha-Varshan* in 1854. It too was published in Calcutta.

Meanwhile the government was becoming aware of the increasing influence of the press and armed itself with powers to control it. The first of these measures, the Press Act of 1857, was designed to regulate the establishment of printing presses. No press could be set up without the previous sanction of the government, and government could prohibit the circulation of any paper which in its view brought it into contempt or hatred. A subsequent Act in 1908 contended that publications in the oriental languages contained matters likely to excite disaffection and to create hatred between different races, castes and religions, 'when read by ignorant and unintelligent persons'. Other measures were taken to tighten government's control over the press culminating in the Press Act of 1910 which gave the government the power to demand an additional security deposit if it appeared to them that the press was being misused in any manner. The Indian Press Association, which was founded in 1915 to protect the interests of the Press, pointed out that up to 1917 twenty-two papers had been called upon to furnish security, and eighteen o them had closed down rather than function in such circumstances.

In 1885 the Indian National Congress was founded through the exertions of an Englishman, Alan Octavian Hume, and thereafter the freedom and development of the Press were largely bound up with what happened in the nationalist movement and the impact of three outstanding leaders: Gopal Krishna Gokhale (1866-1915), the Moderate; Bal Gangadhar Tilak (1856-1920), the militant Hindu nationalist; and Mahatma Gandhi (1869-1948). Gokhale, who was one of the founders of the Marathi paper the 'Sudharkar' (Reformer) at the beginning of the twentieth century, spent his life crusading for, among other things, the freedom of the Indian press. In 1903, while opposing an amendment to the Official Secrets Act which sought to bring within its orbit civil as well as military matters, Gokhale said:

> The vigilance of the Press is the only check which operates from outside, feebly it is true but continuously, on the conduct of the government which is subject to popular control... The Press is in one sense, like the government, a custodian of public interest and any attempt to hamper its freedom is bound to affect these interests prejudicially and cannot fail in the end to react on the position of the government itself.

Tilak, who also opposed various restrictions placed on the Press, was prosecuted for sedition in 1908 and sentenced to a fine of one thousand rupees and six years transportation, which he spent in Mandalay. Tilak appreciated, more than most others, the political importance of mass contact and was somewhat critical of his contemporary journalists for always wanting to play safe.

Gandhiji had used a newspaper, *Indian Opinion*, to express his views while he was in South Africa. Shortly after his arrival on the Indian scene in 1915 he founded two papers to propagate his views. These were *Young India* in English, subsequently known as the *Harijan*, and *Nav Jiwan* in Hindustani. Gandhiji was against advertising in the press since he considered most advertisements indecent and a form of indirect taxation. He believed further that English newspapers reached only a fringe of the population. While it was necessary to use English, especially for the south, till a national language was developed, he had no use for a paper which could not pay its way. On the freedom of the press he was emphatic. In 1920 he told editors that he hoped they would not be daunted by the Press Act. He thought that the press should become fearless, defy consequences and publicise ideas, even when it was in disagreement with them just for the purpose of securing this freedom. Two years later, referring to the government's repressive measures on individual freedom, he wrote:

> I believe that an Editor who has anything worth saying and who commands a clientele cannot be easily hushed as long as his body is left free... Let us use the machine and the type, whilst we can, to give unfettered expression to our thoughts. But let us not feel helpless when they are taken away from us by a 'paternal' government. But the handwritten newspaper is, I admit, a heroic remedy for heroic times.

Several important papers today are over a hundred years old, including the *Malayala Manorama*, the *Amrita Bazar Patrika*, the *Statesman*, the *Times of India*, the *Tribune* and the *Hindu*.

At the end of 1982 the total number of newspapers published in the country was just under 20,000 of which 1384 were dailies. 30.8 per cent of the papers were published from the four cities of Delhi, Bombay, Madras and Calcutta. The largest number of papers were published in Hindi, the next largest being in English, Bengali and Urdu respectively. The total circulation of newspapers has been assessed at 50 million. The highest circulation was for papers in Hindi with English following as a close second. In 1982, 64 per cent of the papers were owned by individuals, 17.5 per cent by societies and associations and 3.4 per cent by the central and state governments. The rest are owned by public or private companies, educational institutions, international organisations, political parties and the like.

There are four news agencies in the country. The Press Trust of India (PTI) and the United News of India (UNI) provide services in English while Samachar Bharati and Hindustan Samachar are Hindi language services. The four services were amalgamated into a single service, 'Samachar,' during the Emergency. The earlier position has since been restored.

Relations between the press and the government immediately after independence were cordial but various strains and stresses have developed since. The most fundamental is in regard to restrictions on the freedom of the press. For while articles 19(1) of the Constitution guarantees freedom of speech and expression, clause (2) states that:

Nothing shall effect the operation of any existing law or prevent the state from making any law, in so far as such law imposes reasonable restrictions on the exercise of the right conferred by the said such sub-clause, in the interests of the sovereignty and integrity of India, the security of the state, friendly relations with foreign states, public order, decency or morality, or in relation to contempt of court, defamation or incitement to an offence.

In 1952 the government set up a Press Commission with wide terms of reference which included among other matters the control and ownership of newspapers, the working of monopolies and chains, the distribution of advertisements and Press and government relations. The Commission reported in 1954. While the government did eventually set up a Press Council which would adjudicate in disputes between the newspapers and state governments and would deal with other matters affecting the newspaper industry and working journalists, it proved to be generally ineffective, and was abolished during the Emergency (26 June 1975 to March 1977) when press censorship was imposed. The Janata government, in 1978, set up a second Press Commission to review the situation. The Congress party which gained a majority in the elections in January 1980 decided to reconstitute the Press Commission and to enlarge its terms of reference. This, known as the Second Press Commission, submitted its report in 1982. The Press Council has been revived as recommended by the Commission.

The Film Industry

India now produces the largest number of feature films of any country in the world. In 1984, 833 films were certified for public exhibition as against 741 in the previous year. Of the total number of films, 515 were produced in Madras, 217 in Bombay and 61 in Calcutta. Feature films are produced entirely in the private sector, but short films are produced both by private producers and also on behalf of the central government and the States. Weekly Indian News Reviews, cartoon films, quickies and documentaries for public information and education are produced by the Films Division of the Ministry of Information and Broadcasting.

The largest number of feature films are in Telugu, Hindi, Tamil, Malayalam, Kannada and Bengali respectively. The total number of cinemas in the country in 1984 was 12 thousand, of which approximately 4,500 were touring cinemas.

The first Indian film, *Rajah Harishchandra* was produced by Dadasaheb Phalke in 1912 and was released a year later, but as far back as 7 July 1896 residents of Bombay were invited by an advertisement in the *Times of India* to witness 'living photographic pictures in life size reproductions by Messrs Lumiere Brothers'. On the same day, another Lumiere exhibition was being witnessed by the Czar in St Petersburg and only a few months previously similar exhibitions had been held in New York and the capital cities of several European states. In India the second city to hold a cinematographic exhibition was Calcutta.

In the early days, the films exhibited in India were produced in the United States, England, France and Germany. The shows took place in hired theatre halls or in tents. Tickets ranged from two rupees to four annas (a quarter of a rupee) for sitting space on the floor. There were separate enclosures for women to witness the shows in purdah, that is, an area screened off from male eyes. An important event in the exhibition of films in India was a 'bioscope' show organised by a J.F. Madan in the Maidan (a wide open field in the heart of Calcutta). This took place in 1902. Subsequently, Madan Theatres Ltd were responsible for a chain of cinema houses in the big cities of India.

Meanwhile an enterprising young Maharashtrian, Harishchandra Sakharam Bhatvadekar, had imported a movie camera for the princely sum of twenty-one guineas. He began by making a film of a wrestling match and another on the training of circus monkeys. He also made the first newsreels of public events, such as the ceremonies held in 1903 in connection with the coronation of

Edward VII. Bhatvadekar's shorts were shown together with the foreign films.

However the first full-length Indian feature film had to await the arrival of Dhundiraj Govind Phalke, better known as Dadasaheb Phalke (1870-1944). Phalke came from a priestly family who lived in a small town near Bombay. He had studied art and photography and had set up an art printing press when he was lured by cinema. He picked up some elementary knowledge on film-making from books, acquired a camera and other essential equipment, and crossed many hurdles to set about his life's mission, that is to produce films based on mythological stories which were part of the tradition and culture of the common man. In 1912 *Rajah Harishchandra* was completed and several others followed, including *The Legend of Bahasmasum*, *Savitri* and the *Birth of Krishna*. Phalke has been described as a special-effects genius. Erik Barnouw and S. Krishnaswamy in their well-known work *Indian Film*, say of Phalke:

> He explored a vast range of techniques, including animation. He experimented with colour, via tinting and toning. He used scenic models for a number of sequences, including the burning of Lanka, for which he also burned down two full sized sets... Having determined the right timing for the printing of a sequence, he set a metronome going to guide his wife; she turned the handle of the printer in time with the metronome. (*Indian Film* by Barnouw and Krishnaswamy).

Phalke was also imbued with a social mission. The performing arts, especially music, dance and drama, which in the past had enjoyed royal patronage, had fallen into disrepute and were almost the exclusive preserve of prostitutes. No respectable woman, and not even a prostitute for that matter, was prepared to play the feminine lead in Phalke's first film. So he had to hire a young man to play the part and he became a great favourite. But later, Phalke's own daughter helped him out and other women from educated backgrounds participated in his films.

World War I was a temporary damper on the growth of the Indian film industry. But from the twenties it did not look back, even in the face of considerable competition from foreign distributors, particularly of American films. In 1926-27, for example, only 15 per cent of the films released were Indian. Import duty on raw film stock was a major constraint.

The thirties heralded a new era for Indian films. The first Indian 'talkie,' *Alam Ara* (Light of the World) was released in 1931. The film was in Hindi, directed by Ardeshir M. Israni, and produced by a company known as the Imperial Company which had acquired sound equipment, described as junk, mainly in the United States. *Alam Ara*, whatever its artistic merits, established once and for all the supremacy of the Indian film for mass appeal as against foreign competitors. Within the year there were twenty-two talkies in Hindi, three in Bengali and one each in Tamil and Telugu; Marathi and Gujarati films followed next year.

Three important film-producing companies were established — the Prabhat Film Company in Poona (1929), New Theatres Ltd. in Calcutta (1930) and Bombay Talkies (1934) — which were to dominate the Indian film world for nearly two decades. The personalities who headed these films were Indians of the highest calibre, V. Shantaram of Prabhat, B.N. Sircar of New Theatres and Himangsu Rai and Devika Rani of Bombay Talkies. Very different from each other, they nevertheless shared the ability to discover talented directors, actors and musicians and they paid great attention to technical quality. Each company was like a family concern and every one worked every day whether he had an assignment or not. The most glamorous of these personalities was undoubtedly Devika Rani, grand-niece of Tagore, who had been mainly educated in England. Her first film *Karma* (Fate) in which she acted opposite Himangsu Rai, released in London in 1933, was a tremendous success. The British press wrote enthusiastically about her 'large velvety eyes [which] can express emotion,' about her gestures, all of which 'speak' and of the perfection of her English. By the fifties the impetus given to the Indian film industry by these pioneers had played itself out and the companies ceased to exist. Songs, dances and the star system were to dominate the Indian cinema.

Indian films and especially Hindi films, are tremendously popular, particularly in the urban areas. In the larger cities there are four shows a day and long queues can be seen outside the booking offices. It has been estimated that films command an audience as many as ten million a day. Critics contend that Indian cinema is largely escapist. It draws on mythology, crime and social themes and in dealing with the latter upholds traditional values without coming to grips with the conflict between tradition and modernity. There are, of course, notable exceptions, the most distinguished being the director Satyajit Ray, a world figure. There are also a number of younger directors and actors producing what are described as the new-wave films such as Mrinal Sen, Girish Karnad, Shyam Benegal and M.S. Sathyu, who are also gaining international fame. It is interesting to observe that thirty years after he produced his famous *Pather Panchali,* Satyajit Ray still has difficulty in obtaining finance and finding distributors to release his films in India. Many of the new-wave films have been financed by the Film Finance Corporation of India which was set up under government aegis in 1966. The main objective of the Corporation is to provide financial assistance to talented young directors and to free them from the financial stranglehold of distributors who insist that films should be made in accordance with a formula that ensures success at the box office.

But whatever the critics may say, one point is conceded by all. The Hindi film has done more to spread the national language throughout the country than any other agency. In the four states of South India, in Bengal and in the northeastern hill states where opposition to Hindi is pronounced, Hindi films are very popular.

The Indian film has developed its own brand of music. It is known as film music and consists of sentimental songs, sometimes bordering on the vulgar. The music is a hybrid of Indian and Western elements, where the singer is supported by what is known as an 'orchestra' — a couple of dozen instruments, strings, wind and percussion, Indian and Western. The harmonisations which precede and intersperse the stanzas of the lyric, bear little relation to the melody. Film music is extremely popular and is affecting the character of all forms of light and folk music in the country. Responsible critics believe that film music is one of the prime factors in corrupting taste. Dr Keskar, who was Minister for Information and Broadcasting for nearly a decade beginning in 1951, virtually banned the broadcast of film music on the ground that it is vulgar in form and content. But this policy had to be modified because it cost the broadcasting organisation too much in popularity. Today, film music dominates the commercial channels of AIR and the influence of the films on music, drama and the whole conception of entertainment in radio and TV is a major factor to be reckoned with. The various influences of the film on radio and TV will be discussed at the appropriate places in this study.

Films are released for public exhibition only after they have been certified by the Central Board of Film Censors which was set up under the Cinematograph (Censorship) Act of 1952. The Board consists of a Chairman and nine members, all of whom are appointed by the Government of India. The Board functions not only in Bombay, which is its headquarters, but also in Madras and Calcutta.

Censorship of films in India was introduced as long ago as 1918 when the Indian Cinematograph Act came into existence. This legislation placed the control of cinemas and censorship within the jurisdiction of the British Indian provinces. Censorship was treated as a reserved subject, which meant that it fell within the purview of the governor and was outside the jurisdiction of the provincial legislative council. In practice it was dealt with by the police department. Since censorship was a provincial subject, no uniform standards were applied, and film sequences approved in one part of the country were banned in others, not to mention the fact that policemen were hardly likely to be sensitive to artistic merit. In the pre-independence period, many of the problems of censorship were connected with newsreels and documentaries depicting the freedom movement. Others related to scenes which were allegedly derogatory to the British rulers or could create tension between religious communities. Thus when after independence, film censorship was brought under a Central Board, the move was widely welcomed by the film industry. Nevertheless, criticism of the government's handling of film censorship has continued, particularly over the questions of sex, prohibition and violence. For example, there has been much public discussion over the question of kissing, which is not allowed in Indian films. It has been argued that kissing in public is un-Indian. On the other hand, kissing is permitted in foreign films which are shown in India. This double standard has come in for a lot of criticism. Again since there is prohibition in various parts of the country, people cannot be shown drinking alcohol. This applies even to foreign films. You can show a person pouring himself a drink, but there is a cut which removes the frames when the glass reaches the lips!

The government of India in a bid to promote artistic excellence in Indian films instituted a National Film Festival in 1953. There are now twenty-six categories of awards, all-India and regional awards included. The regional awards are meant for films produced in the regional languages. In 1980, ninety feature films and one hundred short films competed for the awards. India has held ten competitive International Film Festivals, and four non-competitive International Film Festivals upto 1984. The National and International Film Festivals are organised by a Directorate of Film Festivals which has been set up in the Ministry of Information and Broadcasting in New Delhi.

A Children's Film Society to produce films for children was set up in 1955. There is an active film society movement which started in Calcutta in 1947 through the efforts of the distinguished director Satyajit Ray and Chidananda Dasgupta, a well-known film critic and author of several books on the Indian films.

Indian films are exported to a hundred countries in the world and are popular not only with immigrant Indian populations. In recent years the USSR has emerged as an important buyer of Indian films. On an average about eighty Indian films, most of them in Hindi, are exported annually. Till the end of December 1984, the country earned over 50 million rupees through the export of Indian films. The Government believes that there is a good deal of smuggling of Indian films out of the country and steps have been taken from time to time to plug the loopholes.

The Evolution of Broadcasting 2

A mateur broadcasting started in India in November 1923 with the setting up of a Radio Club in Calcutta. In June 1924 similar clubs in Bombay and Madras began transmitting programmes for some two and a half hours a day. Due to financial difficulties the Madras Club closed down in October 1927. But on 23 July of that year, the first regular radio broadcasts commenced at Bombay and on 26 August a station started functioning in Calcutta.

These stations were started by the Indian Broadcasting Company which had received a licence from the government. Lord Irwin, the Viceroy, who inaugurated the Bombay station, spoke of the needs which broadcasting could serve in words which remain true today, over fifty years later. He said:

> India offers special opportunities for the development of broadcasting. Its distances and wide spaces alone make it a promising field. In India's remote villages there are many who, after the day's work is done, find time hangs heavily enough upon their hands, and there must be many officials and others whose duties carry them into out-of-the-way places where they crave for the company of their friends and the solace of human companionship. There are of course, too, in many house-holds those whom social custom debars from taking part in recreation outside their own homes. To all these and many more broadcasting will be a blessing and a boon of real value. Both for entertainment and for education its possibilities are great, and as yet we perhaps scarcely realise how great they are.

The Indian Broadcasting Company commenced operation with a meagre capital of only one and a half million rupees. Approximately four hundred and fifty thousand rupees was spent on the installation of the two stations. The revenue of the company was derived from two sources. First, it received 80 percent of its revenue from radio licences. The fee was fixed by government at ten rupees per radio set per annum. The company had to collect the licence fees annually from those who possessed the receivers. When the company started, there were less than a thousand radio sets. By the end of 1929 the number had risen only to 7,775. In 1930, however, the number of licences registered a decrease. The second source of revenue for the company was a ten per cent 'tribute' on the invoiced value of imported wireless equipment such as receivers, wireless valves, electric wireless gramophones, which the company itself had to collect from the dealers.

The monthly expenditure of the company was considerably in excess of its revenue. The company, therefore, reduced its expenditure. The fall in licences after 1929 made it clear that the company would not be in a position to carry on unless it received more funds. An application for a loan made to the government was turned down. As a result the company went into liquidation in June 1930.

Various reasons have been given for the fall in licences and the failure of the Indian Broadcasting Company. Fielden in his Report contends that the company did not have sufficient capital to start with. It had problems in collecting the 'tribute' and the licence fee. The price of a four-valve radio set was Rs 500 which was considered very high. Finally, he argued that in India, barring the cities of Bombay and Calcutta, there was apathy towards art forms such as music and theatre, and at any rate, channels for bringing them before the public did not exist. This contention has been hotly disputed. If there were no centres for exposure, India could not have developed highly sophisticated systems of music, dance, theatre and other art forms. H.R. Luthra, in his recent historical study *Indian Broadcasting* (1986), points out that the programmes of the IBC catered to the small European community and westernised Indians. There was little effort to reach out to the vast majority of the people and there was no publicity for the new medium.

Meanwhile, several representations had been made for some positive action by the government. The leaders of the political parties in the Central Assembly had taken up the matter with the Minister for Labour and Industry and urged that the service should be continued without interruption. Fielden, to whom we must be grateful for information about the early history of Indian broadcasting, writes in his *Report to the Government* which was submitted in 1939, that the Government of India decided to take over the service on the following conditions — as Fielden puts it:

(a) Government to acquire the Bombay and Calcutta stations of the company, subject to it being possible for them to do this at a purchase price which represented no more than the actual depreciated value of the assets;

(b) to take over the staff of the company on their existing terms;

(c) to run the concern experimentally through the Department of Labour and Industries for two years in the first instance, during which the estimated expenditure was to be Rs. 267,000 per annum against an anticipated revenue of Rs. 126,000 leaving a deficit of Rs. 141,000 per annum to be met from the revenues of the Government of India.

Detailed proposals to acquire and run broadcasting stations were approved by the Standing Finance Committee of Government on 24 February 1930, and broadcasting came under its direct control in the Department of Labour and Industries on 1 April, 1930. It was designated the Indian State Broadcasting Service. An Advisory Committee was set up to advise on the management and expansion of the service. The Indian State Broadcasting Service took over the assets and liabilities of the company. The collection of the annual licence fee became the responsibility of the Posts and Telegraphs department. The money collected was, in accordance with the general procedure in the Government of India, credited to the Consolidated Fund of India. A percentage of this amount, around 10 per cent originally, was shown as collection charges and credited by a book adjustment to the Posts and Telegraphs Department. The remaining amount was also by a book entry shown as a credit to the Indian State Broadcasting Service. The monies collected by the Customs Department were likewise credited to the Consolidated Fund of India, but they were not acknowledged, as the licence fee was as monies earned by broadcasting. This situation continued till 1985 when the licencing system was abolished.

Between 1930 and 1935 Indian broadcasting was in the doldrums. Financial stringency kept the services at a very low level. During this period two important steps were taken to make the service self-supporting. By the Indian Tariff (Wireless Broadcasting) Amendment Act of 1932, the duty on wireless receiving apparatus was doubled and fixed at 50 percent. In the following year the Indian Wireless

Telegraphy Act came into being which made the possession of a radio set without a licence an offence. The earlier Act — The Indian Telegraphy Act of 1885 — had given power to government to control the establishment, maintenance and working of wireless apparatus but the mere possession of wireless apparatus or radio receivers had not come within its purview and the collection of licence fees had constituted a major problem for the company.

These measures improved the financial situation of the Indian State Broadcasting Service and government started thinking of expanding the department. Meanwhile the Government of India Act 1935 had come into existence. The constitutional position of broadcasting was defined in Section 129 of the Act as follows:

(1) The Federal Government shall not unreasonably refuse to entrust to the Government of any Province or the Ruler of any Federated State such functions with respect to broadcasting as may be necessary to enable that Government or Ruler,

    (a) to construct and use transmitters in the Province or State;

    (b) to regulate, and impose fees in respect of the construction and use of transmitters and use of receiving apparatus in the Province or State.

Provided that nothing in this sub-section shall be construed as requiring the Federal Government to entrust to any such Government or Ruler any control over the use of transmitters constructed or maintained by the Federal Government or by persons authorised by the Federal Government, or over the use of receiving apparatus by persons so authorised.

(2) Any functions so entrusted to a Government or Ruler shall be exercised subject to such conditions as may be imposed by the Federal Government, including, notwithstanding anything in this Act, any conditions with respect to finance, but it shall not be lawful for the Federal Government so to impose any conditions regulating the matter broadcast by, or by authority of, the Government or Ruler.

(3) Nothing in this section shall be construed as restricting the powers conferred on the Governor-General by this Act for the prevention of any grave menace to the peace and tranquillity of India, or as prohibiting the imposition on

Government or Rulers of such conditions regulating matter broadcast as appear to be necessary to enable the Governor-General to discharge his functions in so far as he is by or under this Act required in the exercise thereof to act in his discretion or to exercise his individual judgement.

To further the development of broadcasting the government acquired the services of Lionel Fielden of the BBC. He came out to India in August 1935 and assumed charge as Controller of Broadcasting. The central station at Delhi was inaugurated on New Year's Day of 1936. Fielden felt that he needed the assistance of a technical expert to help him in drawing up plans for the expansion of radio. Thus H.L. Kirke, a distinguished BBC research engineer, came to India on 23 January 1936. Together they drew up a plan which was adopted with modifications after the appointment of a Chief Engineer, Mr C.W. Goyder, also of the BBC, who assumed charge in August.

All India Radio*

In June 1935 the designation Indian State Broadcasting Service was changed to All India Radio. How this came about is graphically described by Fielden in his autobiography, *The Natural Bent* (1960):

> I had never liked the title ISBS (Indian State Broadcasting Service) which to me seemed not only unwieldy but also tainted with officialdom. After a good deal of cogitation — which may seem ridiculous now, but these apparently simple and obvious things do not always appear easily — I had concluded that All India Radio would give me not only protection from the clauses which I most feared in the 1935 Act, but would also have the suitable initials AIR. I worked out a monogram which placed these letters over the map of India, and it is now about the only thing which remains of me in India. But when I mooted this point, I found that there was immense opposition in the Secretariat to any such

* Since 1936 the Government of India's monopoly broadcasting organisation has been known as All India Radio (AIR). AIR is registered as such in the Asia – Pacific Broadcasting Union (ABU) and in the Commonwealth Broadcasting Association (CBA). The alternative name, mainly used within India, is Akashvani (literally 'cosmic voice').

change. They wanted ISBS and they thought it fine. I realised that I must employ a little unnatural tact. I cornered Lord Linlithgow after a Viceregal banquet, and said plaintively that I was in a great difficulty and needed his advice. (He usually responded well to such an opening). I said I was sure that he agreed with me that ISBS was a clumsy title. After a slight pause, he nodded his long head wisely. Yes, it was rather a mouthful. I said that perhaps it was a pity to use the word broadcasting at all, since all Indians had to say 'brodcasting' — 'broad' was for them an unpronounceable word. But I could not, I said, think of another title: could he help me? 'Indian State', I said, was a term which, as he well knew, hardly fitted into the 1935 Act. It should be something general. He rose beautifully to the bait. "All India?" I expressed my astonishment and admiration. The very thing. But surely not "Broadcasting"? After some thought he suggested "radio"?. Splendid, I said — and what beautiful initials: The Viceroy concluded that he had invented it and there was no more trouble. His pet name must be adopted. Thus All India Radio was born.

In 1937 AIR was transferred from the Ministry of Labour and Industries to the Department of Communications; and in 1941 to a new department of Information and Broadcasting which after Independence became a Ministry in 1947.

The basic structure for the AIR network devised by Fielden and Kirke, as modified by Goyder, was to set up medium-wave radio stations at some principal centres which would provide a good ground wave signal within a reasonable radius. The central station at Delhi would additionally be provided with short-wave transmitters, thereby linking it with the other stations. Short-wave transmitters would be established at Bombay, Calcutta and Madras to give second grade service to remoter areas. Basically this ground plan has survived over the forty odd years since it was conceived. In the years immediately following, six new stations including Madras came on the air. In the states ruled by Indian princes, stations were also set up at Baroda, Mysore and Trivandrum, Hyderabad and Aurangabad.

In the early years other events occurred which have been of significance in the development of All India Radio. First, in 1935 private stations were set up in Peshawar in the North-West Frontier Province and in Allahabad in the United Provinces which started broadcasting programmes for rural audiences. These stations, later incorporated into the AIR network, mark the beginnings of the Rural Programmes which are now an important component in its output.

Second, in 1937 the Central News Organisation (now known as the News Services Division) came into existence. Before this, news summaries had been broadcast from some stations but news bulletins and commentaries were not prepared on a professional basis.

Third, AIR, in 1939, started broadcasting to foreign audiences. The first such broadcast was in Pushto and was addressed to listeners in Afghanistan. External broadcasts expanded rapidly under the impact of World War II, when many of these services were the joint responsibility of AIR and the Far Eastern Bureau of the British Ministry of Information. The External Services of AIR are now broadcasting fifty-seven hours a day in some twenty-five languages, including six Indian languages, and in English.

Fielden left India in 1940 to aid in the war effort and his place as head of All India Radio, was taken by Professor A.S.Bokhari. (The designation Controller of Broadcasting was changed to Director-General in 1943). Prof Bokhari guided the affairs of AIR for six years. A brilliant intellectual and belletrist, he combined with these gifts the qualities of a fair and clear-sighted administrator. It was he who established the zest for inquiry, and standards of artistic excellence and efficiency for which AIR was known in its early days. After Partition he opted for Pakistan and rendered distinguished service to that country at the United Nations.

When India was partitioned in August 1947, the AIR network consisted of six stations and there were five stations in the princely states. The total number of licences was 248,000. Immediately after 1947 a scheme for the development of broadcasting, known as the Pilot Project, was drawn up. The intention was to set up studios with a lower power medium wave transmitter in each distinct linguistic and cultural region in the country. For a start the objective was to establish one radio station in each state. Subsequently in 1951, with the commitment of the country to centralised planning, AIR's expansion has been included in the government's successive Five Year Plans. The Plans are discussed further in chapter 3.

Rural Broadcasting

Reference has already been made to rural programmes and their place in AIR's programme schedules. After the incorporation of the

Peshawar and Allahabad rural services into AIR, it became part of the general pattern that each station should broadcast a half hour special programme for rural audiences. This was a composite compered programme which included a weather report, market prices, talks and discussions on agriculture, animal husbandry, crafts, health and hygiene. Folk music provided light relief.

Attempts were also made to provide community listening sets in the villages. While this was left to the initiative of the provincial governments in the pre-Independence period, Community Listening was included as part of the Five Year Plan after 1950. The arrangement was that the centre would make itself responsible for providing 50 per cent of the expenditure incurred by a state government for installing community radio sets in the villages. The state governments were, however, expected to maintain the sets. Since electricity was not available in most of the villages, batteries had to be replaced at regular intervals and repairs had to be carried out whenever the sets went out of order. This scheme had a limited success, although by 1965-66 the number of community receivers had gone up to 150,000. The major problem was regular replacement of batteries and maintenance. However, community listening has been overtaken by the transistor revolution and by 1970 the scheme was withdrawn. It continues to function under AIR in Jammu and Kashmir, and in a few other states at the initiative of their respective governments.

A major departure in rural programming was made in 1956 when, with the assistance of UNESCO, an experiment in Radio Rural Forums was conducted at the Poona station. (Poona is now referred to as Pune but the earlier name has been retained as this is the name mentioned in the UNESCO Report on this experiment). The intention of the forums was to establish two-way communication between agricultural audiences on the one hand and programme organisers and producers on the other. A detailed discussion of this topic is given in chapter 4.

News Services

Between 1930 and 1936 AIR's Bombay amd Calcutta stations, and Delhi when the station came on the air in 1936, were broadcasting two daily news bulletins in the peak period 2030 to 2130; one bulletin in English, the second in Hindustani from Bombay and Delhi and in

Bengali from Calcutta. Each station produced its own bulletins. The stations experimented with the placing of further daily bulletins but it was not until 1937 when the Central News Organisation (CNO) was created that these were established at 1800 in English and 1805 in Hindustani.

Hindustani signifies a mixture of Hindi and Urdu, a language of the streets, in which AIR broadcast news bulletins until 1949. Defending Hindustani as the main language of broadcasting Fielden commented in his *Report,* that AIR had 'tentatively adopted it as a language spoken or at least understood in the greater part of Aryan-speaking India.' Recognising the difficulties of achieving maximum intelligibility he went on to say, 'There is, however, a feeling in the country that All India Radio should assist in the evolution and expansion of a common language for India, and it is in pursuance of this feeling, no less than for practical considerations, that All India Radio is endeavouring to widen the scope of Hindustani.' Interestingly enough, Gandhiji had advocated Hindustani — written in either the Devanagiri script used for Hindi or the Persian script used for Urdu — as the national language of India but he was outvoted by the pundits. Hindustani continued to be used for a short while after Independence. On 27 November 1949, AIR's programme journals substituted the word Hindi for Hindustani. Shortly afterwards separate newscasts started in Urdu. Today Hindustani is not officially recognised as a language.

Two schemes for the broadcast of news from the stations were considered when the CNO was to start: a centralised scheme for the preparation of news scripts at a central news room in Delhi which would then be relayed to the stations by telephone live or off the air, and an alternative plan for each station to prepare and edit its own news bulletins. The first scheme was adopted in the interests of centralised control and of economy. The idea of supplementing centralised bulletins by regional bulletins originating at the stations had to wait for implementation till 1953 when a beginning was made to set up Regional News Units at selected stations. While the relay of central bulletins through telephone lines was unsatisfactory, the provision of high power short-wave transmitters improved matters. This pattern of off-air relay for the central bulletins has continued ever since.

At the initial stages the Central News Organisation had no arrangements of its own for news collection. Senior members of the editorial staff were deputed for reporting assignments on special occasions. However, in 1945 a Reporting Unit was set up and a few posts of Assistant News Reporter and Reporter were created. It was in June 1945 that AIR undertook its first major reporting assignment in connection with a Conference called in Simla by the Viceroy, Lord Wavell, to discuss with Indian leaders proposals for the next step in the country's progress towards self-government. After the conclusion of hostilities in Asia, AIR appointed its first foreign correspondents who were assigned to China, Indonesia and with the Allied Occupation Force in Japan. The news-gathering activities of AIR have expanded considerably since.

External Services

AIR's External Services developed under the impact of World War II and were initially part of the Central News Organisation. External broadcasts, as already mentioned, started in October 1939 with a broadcast in Pushtu directed at Afghanistan. With the advance of the Axis powers in West Asia and South East Asia and their propaganda offensives in these parts, the British government thought it necessary to take counter-measures. This was done by coordination of foreign broadcasts through the Far Eastern Bureau of the British Ministry of Information and AIR. The foreign broadcasts were organised under two different categories. There were broadcasts which were directed to Indians overseas in a number of Indian languages. These were controlled by an Indian Political Warfare section. The well-known Indian writer Nirad Chaudhuri was among the first persons to be recruited to write commentaries in this section. The second group consisted of broadcasts in various languages addressed to foreign nations in South Asia and the Middle East. The core of the programme was a news bulletin, a commentary and music. In recognition of its dual function, the Central News Organisation was redesignated as the Office of the Director of News and External Services. By 1945 AIR was putting out seventy-four daily broadcasts in twenty-two languages.

With the end of the war, the arrangement with the Far Eastern Bureau ceased and the number of daily external broadcasts was reduced. By 31 March 1947 the number of daily external broadcasts had come down to thirty-one. The External Services were separated from the News Services in 1949 and constituted as a distinctive service. The services were also remodelled. But the basic distinction between services addressed to Indian audiences overseas in Indian languages and to foreign nationals in various languages has continued.

Vividh Bharati — The Commercial Service

Reference has been made in the first chapter to film music and its virtual ban on AIR. In 1952 the Minister for Information and Broadcasting, B.V. Keskar, who was an enthusiastic admirer of classical music, described film music as cheap and vulgar. Instructions were issued to stations to screen both the text of the lyrics and the music and to approve for broadcast only such records which were in conformity with good taste. This offended the Film Producers Associations, and many of them terminated their contracts with AIR. Very little film music was broadcast and this militated against the popularity of AIR. Meanwhile, Radio Ceylon on its Commercial Service started beaming programmes to various parts of India consisting mainly of Indian film hits. This made Radio Ceylon very popular and it drew away a large number of listeners in the country. In order to combat this competition AIR introduced a new service in 1957 which was known as Vividh Bharati or the All India Variety Programme (AIVP) channel. Originally programmes on Vividh Bharati were radiated on two high-power short-wave transmitters at Bombay and Madras. After 1960 the programme has been made progressively available on low-power medium-wave transmitters.

Vividh Bharati programmes, whether of music or the spoken word, were presented in Hindi. Approximately 85 percent of the transmission consisted of music — film music, light, regional, folk and devotional music. The remainder was taken up by Hindi news bulletins, skits and short features. AIR stations were required to contribute items of music and spoken word on tape to a central office set up in Bombay. Programme staff at the Vividh Bharati centre selected items out of this material and put them together to form the total transmission. Copies of these tapes were prepared on high speed recorders and despatched to the Vividh Bharati channels set up at stations. As the number of channels increased, more copies of the tapes were prepared at the Bombay centre. The Vividh Bharati Programme was thus based almost exclusively on material provided by the stations and it is for this reason that Vividh Bharati is described as a library service.

In 1967 it was decided to progressively commercialise the Vividh Bharati channels. The Government's decision was that advertising time should not exceed a maximum of 10 per cent of the total transmission time. Initially only commercial spots were accepted, but after a few years time was also made available for sponsored programmes.

The commercialisation of Vividh Bharati channels was undertaken in three stages. To begin with the Vividh Bharati channels in Bombay, Nagpur and Poona were commercialised. Three years later similar action was taken in Delhi, Calcutta and Madras which are also important trade and commercial centres. While the available time on the Bombay and Delhi centres was quickly sold out, and there has been and continues to be a long waiting list, the commercial channels in Calcutta and Madras were not equally successful due to a variety of reasons, including political and economic instability in the case of West Bengal.

Subsequently Vividh Bharati channels were commercialised without ascertaining whether there was a sufficient demand. For example channels went commercial in Srinagar (Kashmir), Cuttak (Orissa), Trivandrum (Kerala) and Allahabad (UP) though these are not commercial centres of any significance. The result has been that these and other centres in small towns have not been able to sell the time at their disposal. An important development took place in April 1982. Commercial spots were introduced on the main channel and carried on the entire network immediately before and after the major morning and evening Hindi and English news bulletins.

National and international sports events, sponsored by commercial houses, are also carried on the national network. When the Commercial Service was started, a Central Advisory Committee consisting of representatives of advertising agencies, social scientists and others was set up to advise AIR on various aspects of the service. Advisory Committees were also set up at a few commercial broadcasting centres, such as Delhi. All these committees have lapsed since 1975.

Yuv Vani – The Voice of Youth

A unique experiment was undertaken by AIR when on 23 July 1969, the day on which man first walked on the moon, a special youth service was inaugurated at Delhi. A separate channel was made available to radiate programmes planned, presented, and, as far as possible, managed by young people. A large number of young persons, mainly university students, came forward to participate and have produced first-rate programmes. One such programme, *Echoes of a Generation,* won the ABU prize in 1976. After the success of Yuv Vani in Delhi, similar Yuv Vani channels were started in Calcutta, Hyderabad and Jammu.

The Birth of Television*

Television started in India on 15 September 1959 when AIR's first experimental centre at Delhi was inaugurated by the President. The equipment was given to the Government of India by Philips India Ltd. who had set up closed circuit television at an Industrial Exhibition organised in Delhi. The primary purpose of this pilot project was 'experimentation, training and evaluation'. There were two programmes a week, on Tuesday and Friday evenings, each of one hour.

Initially twenty-one TV sets were installed in the rural areas in the neighbourhood of Delhi. Subsequently UNESCO provided approximately fifty sets which were also installed in the rural areas. Tele-clubs were set up at these community viewing centres.

From 23 December 1960 to 5 May 1961 under UNESCO auspices an experiment in social education was undertaken which has been described in UNESCO's 'Reports and Papers on Mass Communication' No. 38 published in 1963. It says that the programmes were designed to 'add to the information of viewers on various topics, to influence, if possible, their attitudes towards aspects of issues and to encourage follow-up group action and behaviour.' The general theme of the programmes arranged for the experiment was the 'Responsibilities of Citizenship' and the topics covered were traffic and road sense, community health, adulteration of food stuffs, good manners, encroachment on public property, and town planning.

Subsequently an agreement was made by AIR with the Ford Foundation to conduct an experiment in in-school teaching through TV. Two hundred and fifty sets were installed in higher secondary schools in Delhi and eight lessons each, of a duration of twenty

---

* Television in India has been known as Doordarshan ('distant vision') since its inception. When TV became a department separate from AIR, Doordarshan was registered as an independent member of ABU and CBA under this name.

minutes, were prepared. Each lesson was telecast twice a day, once in the morning and again in the afternoon for the benefit of the second shift in the schools. The subjects covered were Physics, Chemistry, Hindi, English, Current Affairs and Geography. The programmes were jointly prepared by the Education Department of the Delhi Administration and AIR.

Thus social education for farmers and educational programmes for children were the initial objectives of experimental TV in India. While the number of community viewing sets went up in Delhi's rural areas and in schools, and AIR's TV transmissions were slowly extended, some thirteen years were to pass before AIR's second TV centre was established at Bombay in 1972. This hesitation in promoting TV needs to be explained since the doubts then raised continue to dog the development of TV in India.

The basic point was that since TV is expensive it is widely considered a luxury. Jawaharlal Nehru, for example, often expressed this view and argued that India could not afford such an expensive toy. At the same time he contended that the potentialities of radio had not been fully exploited. The counter-argument was that TV could be a powerful weapon for social change and it should be used for such a purpose and not to provide yet another medium for the entertainment of the rich. Thus the accepted raison d'être for the introduction and expansion of TV in India has been to provide a medium for the education of the socially deprived. Unfortunately the government has done little to provide community viewing sets in the villages. This, coupled with the high cost of a receiver, has in fact meant that the vast majority of viewers are in the middle or higher income groups in the cities and for this audience sophisticated programmes and entertainment are the prime consideration.

The second TV centre was inaugurated in Bombay on 2 October 1972 and centres were opened in Srinagar (Kashmir) and Amritsar in the Punjab, the following year. The setting up of these centres was the direct result of developments across the border in Pakistan, which had stations in Lahore and Islamabad, whose programmes were being seen by growing numbers of viewers in India! In the Kashmir valley some two hundred and fifty TV receivers were located in the villages for community viewing.

A most important year for the development of TV in India was 1975. Centres were opened in Calcutta on 9 August, in Madras on 14 August and in November a TV centre was established in Lucknow.

Two of the centres were makeshift arrangements. In Calcutta an old and disused film studio was renovated and set up for use, with the equipment from an OB Van providing the control panel. In Lucknow a single studio with a control room and tele-cine arrangements was hastily rigged up. In Madras alone was there a proper studio building with three studios, control room, tele-cine and office accommodation. Madras remains the only TV centre which is housed in a building designed and constructed for the purpose. All the others are working in old buildings which have been adapted to meet minimum needs.

In April 1976 Doordarshan, AIR's television service, was constituted as a separate department with its own Director-General by Indira Gandhi's government during the period of the Emergency.

The Satellite Instructional Television Experiment (SITE)

A most important event in the history of Indian TV was the Satellite Instructional Television Experiment (SITE) which was conducted between 1 August 1975 and 31 July 1976. In accordance with an agreement signed between the US National Aeronautics and Space Administration (NASA) and the Government of India, the Application Technology Satellite (ATS-6) was used to beam TV signals to 2400 direct reception TV receivers. These receivers were installed in six states with approximately 400 sets in each state or cluster, as it was called. The ordinary domestic receiver was modified by providing what was described as a front-end converter, and a chicken-mesh antenna, rather like an umbrella to look at. This work was done by the Indian Space Research Organisation (ISRO), which was also responsible for setting up and maintaining up-links at Ahmedabad and Delhi. ISRO was in addition responsible for the maintenance of the receivers.

The vast bulk of the programmes was produced by Doordarshan. The programmes were available for some four hours a day — one and a half hours in the morning for an educational programme and two and a half hours for programmes in the evening. The programmes were broadcast for the different clusters in Hindi, Oriya, Telugu and Kannada. Clusters in Bihar, Madhya Pradesh and Rajasthan received programmes in Hindi, those in Orissa, Andhra and Karnataka in Oriya, Telugu and Kannada. There was also a half hour programme in Hindi telecast from Delhi in the evening which was common for all clusters. It included a news bulletin, some item of general interest and a cultural programme. SITE is discussed in detail in chapter 4.

SITE Continuity Centres

Since the satellite had been loaned to India for just one year, the question as to what would happen when the satellite was removed became all important. While some preliminary thinking had already gone into this question, the matter was taken up with considerable energy shortly after the launching of SITE. In any case an Indian satellite would not be available for several years and in the interim period arrangements would have to be made to cover the SITE villages by means of terrestrial transmitters. AIR took the view that this coverage should be integrated with the overall development plans for the extension of TV. Since terrestrial transmitters were inevitable, these together with some studios, should be installed at state capitals. A terrestrial system would provide a service, not only for the community viewing in SITE villages, but also for urban viewers on domestic TV sets. Such a system, it was argued, would be in the overall interests of TV. On the other hand, ISRO argued that low-power transmitters should be set up in the rural areas themselves and they should transmit programmes exclusively for their respective rural audiences. A film recording team should be provided at each transmitter location to prepare local material which would then be sent back for processing and editing at the Base Production Centre. ISRO contended that if the transmitters and production facilities were installed at the urban centres, programme production would be diverted to serving urban interests and the entire raison d'être of SITE would be lost.

In the end ISRO won their case and SITE continuity, as it is termed, is being provided through 100-watt transmitters set up in the rural areas. When the ATS satellite was withdrawn none of these transmitters were ready and for a few months the community viewing centres in all clusters were dead. The first continuity centre came up in March 1977 at Jaipur. Since then six such centres have come into operation and between them they cover forty per cent of SITE villages.

Satellite and Network Programmes

15 August 1982 was an important date in the annals of Doordarshan.

It was the first time that national coverage was provided by Doordarshan through INSAT IA and also for the first time that transmission was in colour. This transmission started in the morning with Prime Minister Indira Gandhi's traditional address to the nation from the Red Fort in Delhi. In the evening, from 8 to 10 PM approximately, commenced the network or national programme which has been telecast daily ever since. When INSAT IA finally failed on 4 September 1982, the relay was carried on with the help of microwave links till INSAT IB became operative.

The Asian Games 1982

The coverage given by Doordarshan to the Ninth Asian Games in November-December 1982 was a milestone in the history of the organisation. Daily telecasts, mostly in colour, were relayed over the forty-one transmitters which then constituted the network. Doordarshan assisted over a dozen organisations of the Asia-Pacific Broadcasting Union and the Arab States Broadcasting Union to prepare their own capsules despatched over Intelsat. Four newly-ordered colour OB vans and five existing black-and-white vans were pressed into service. What was remarkable was the way in which the technical staff fitted up the equipment, received only a few days before the commencement of the Games and how the programme staff used it with hardly any time for testing or familiarisation. Since then there has been an enormous increase in the live coverage of sports and games by Doordarshan.

Expansion of the Doordarshan Network

In July 1983, with barely eighteen months of the Sixth Plan to go, the government sanctioned a gigantic scheme for the expansion of the network involving 680 million rupees. When the scheme was launched there were 45 TV transmitters covering 28 per cent of the population. It was planned to raise the number to 180, the new transmitters being mainly of 100 watts but a few 10-KWT transmitters were to be added. As a result the TV service is available for 52 per cent of the population. All the new transmitting centres relay programmes of the Delhi centre via the satellite INSAT IB.

The Audience

Between the beginnings of broadcasting and 1980 the Posts and

Telegraphs Department issued licences to viewers, collected the revenue and retained 15 per cent as collection charges. It had three classes of licences—for domestic receivers, for receivers in commercial establishments, and in schools. The system applied for both radio and TV. This was much criticised. There was widespread piracy, encouraged to some extent by the cumbersome procedure which among other things required the licence to be renewed at the same Post Office where it had been originally issued. Modifying or abolishing the system altogether had been discussed for two decades, but nothing happened. Then in August 1980 the government abolished licences on single and two-band radio sets and in 1985 licences on radio and TV were completely abolished.

While this came as a relief to listeners and viewers, it made it impossible to gauge with any accuracy the total number of radio sets in the country and their distribution as between urban and rural audiences. The last complete official figures for radio licences pertain to 1979 and put the number of licences at 21 million. The current estimate is 65 million. This figure is based on the number of radio sets being manufactured in the country. Relatively accurate figures can be had from the big manufacturers. However, although some '7 million sets are believed to have been produced in 1982, there was a decline thereafter and production seems to have settled down at around 6.5 million. As there is no glut in the market presumably the radio sets are being sold. Starting with a base estimate, making an allowance for writing off sets which become useless and then adding a figure for the new sets produced and sold we get the current guestimate.

Because of the abolition of the licencing system, the last official figure in respect of TV licence is for 1984. At the end of that year the number of licenced TV sets was 3.6 million. Well over half of these were located in the four metropolitan cities with Bombay leading. It housed over 8,00,000; Delhi had 641,000, Madras 312,000 and Calcutta 262,000. The Directorate-General's current estimate is 7 million TV sets at the end of 1986.

No one is prepared to hazard a guess as to the number of TV sets in the rural areas. As for community viewing sets, official figures are not forthcoming. The Joshi Working Group which enquired into TV software in 1983 said that the figure had never touched the 10,000 mark. By the end of March 1986, 3000 Direct Reception Sets (DRS) are expected to be in the villages of six states where programmes for rural audiences are to be telecast on satellite.

While the licencing system was in force there was some data about the distribution of radio sets in different parts of the country. In 1979, for example there was an average of one set being shared by forty-five persons. There was, however, considerable variation from one state to another. In Karnataka there was one set for twenty-three persons, in Tamilnadu one set for twenty-five, while in Orissa and the Bihar figures were one for eighty-three and one for eighty-nine.

The vast majority of licenced radio receivers were and presumably still are in urban areas, which account for only 20 per cent of the total population. The Posts and Telegraphs Department did not maintain statistics in terms of urban and rural. Precise information on the distribution of radio sets between them has not therefore been available. Estimates made by various research groups are that between 15 and 25 per cent of the total number of sets were in the rural areas. The Information, Planning and Analysis Group of the Electronics Commission was of the view that 20 per cent of the total number of radio sets were in the rural areas.

In 1947 at Partition the total number of radio licences in force in India was 2.75 million. Since then the growth of licence figures has been as follows:

	YEAR	NUMBER OF LICENCES
RADIO	1947	2,750,000
	1950	546,200
	1960	2,128,000
	1970	11,836,000
	1977	20,091,000
	1978	19,611,000
	1979	20,900,000
TV	1970	248,300
	1976	479,020
	1978	899,100
	1980	1,547,918
	1982	2,111,726
	1983	2,800,800
	1984	3,632,328

The Broadcasting System Today: Regulation and Organisation   3

Laws Relating to Broadcasting

According to article 246 of the Indian constitution, Parliament has exclusive powers to make laws with respect to any of the matters enumerated in List I of the seventh schedule. Item 31 in this list reads as follows:

> Posts and telegraphs; telephones, wireless, broadcasts and other like forms of communication.

Thus broadcasting is a central subject and all laws and regulations concerning AIR and Doordarshan emanate exclusively from the government. Two other laws are also of relevance. The first is the Indian Telegraph Act of 1885, which vests in the Government of India the exclusive right to 'establish, maintain and work' wireless apparatus. The monopoly of broadcasting by the government rests on this Act. This Act however did not restrict persons from the mere 'possession' of wireless apparatus. This particular lacuna in the earlier act was redressed by the Indian Wireless Telegraphy Act of 1933. The Indian Wireless Telegraphy (Possession) Rules 1933 regulate the conditions under which receiving sets and equipment may be held in possession by dealers and for domestic use. Licence fees for possession of radio and TV receivers, and for other apparatus for various purposes are determined under these Rules. Apart from the constitutional provision and these two Acts, there are at present no laws regulating broadcasting. Transmission hours depend on production capacity and financial resources. When the Vividh Bharati channel was commercialised in 1967, as recommended by the Chanda Committee, the Cabinet laid down that no more than

10 per cent of the total output of the channel could be devoted to advertisements. This limitation has been observed ever since and has also been followed by Doordarshan which introduced commercials in 1976.

Broadcasting Relations with Government and the Civil Service

The Ministry of Information and Broadcasting is the policy-making body for the broadcasting system today. The Minister is assisted by the Secretary, who is the seniormost civil servant, supported by a massive secretariat divided into wings each under an officer of the rank of Joint Secretary. The three wings are Broadcasting, Information, and Policy and Coordination.

A word is necessary here to explain a basic fact about the personnel policy of the government. The Ministries are manned by officers drawn from the various all-India services of government. The top posts such as Secretary, Additional Secretary, Joint Secretary etc. are almost exclusively held by officers drawn from the Indian Administrative Services (IAS) and posts requiring specialised knowledge of finance and budgeting are the preserve of officers of the Indian Audit and Accounts Service (IA&AS). Intermediate and junior level posts are held by members of the Central Secretariat Service (CSS) or young IAS or IA&AS officers. Thus most posts in the Ministries are held by generalists. In recent years there has been considerable public discussion about this arrangement. It has been argued that unless the higher posts are manned by technocrats and specialists, Indian administration will continue to lack dynamism and be hamstrung by bureaucratic procedures and red tape. In a few of the scientific departments such as Atomic Energy, Science and Technology, Economic Affairs, Agriculture and in the Department of Steel professional persons have been appointed as Secretaries to Government. A few distinguished educationists have in the past held office as Secretary to Government but in more recent times these posts have reverted to the IAS. By and large the hold of the IAS over the top posts continues.

The Ministry of Information and Broadcasting is exclusively manned by generalist officers drawn from the services mentioned above. Of the thirteen Directors-General of All India Radio who have served between 1947 and 1985, seven have been drawn from the ICS (the prestigious Indian Civil Service of British days) and the IAS and six from the programme cadre of AIR.

The Central Information Service was formed in 1960. Government at that stage incorporated within a single cadre staff performing editorial, publicity and public relations work in AIR and in all the other departments of the Ministry of Information and Broadcasting. The main reasons for this step were that the number of officers employed in such duties in the various departments was small, the number of higher posts to which they could aspire was extremely limited and this resulted in stagnation and lack of enterprise.

All India Radio and Doordarshan are two departments or attached offices under the Ministry of Information and Broadcasting. Other departments are the Press Information Bureau, the Publications Division, the Directorate of Advertising and Visual Publicity, the Films Division, and the Song and Drama Division. Radio and TV, however, account for some two-thirds of the Budget of the Ministry and are the most important departments under its control. Thr internal structures of the two departments are similar. AIR being the older and far larger of the two, its structure is more elaborate and the status of its Director-General was till 1984 higher in the Government hierarchy. While the Director-General of AIR has been ranked since 1974 as an Additional Secretary to the Government, his counterpart in Doordarshan was of Joint Secretary status. The engineering head of Doordarshan ranks as a Chief Engineer in the Indian Broadcasting (Engineers) Service, a joint cadre which was formed in 1981. There are about a dozen officers who hold this rank.

Doordarshan was separated from AIR on 1 April 1976 on the ground that TV requires its own specialisation. However, little has been done since then to separate the Programme and Engineering and News Cadres of the two departments. Quite the reverse. The Indian Broadcasting (Engineers) Service came into existence four years ago and the finishing touches are now being given to the Programme Cadre of the service. The main purpose of reorganising the Engineers' Service was to upgrade the scales and bring them on par with other engineering services in the Government of India. Some top designations underwent a change. The Chief Engineer of AIR, the most senior engineer in the two departments, is now designated Engineer-in-Chief; and the next two rungs have become Chief Engineer and Superintending Engineer, replacing three posts designated Additional Chief Engineer, Deputy Chief Engineer and Senior

Engineer. The programme cadre of the Indian Broadcasting Service is to bring about symmetry, so loved by all bureaucracies! However the point in the present context is that the cadres are common to the two services and there have been cases in the last nine years when Senior Engineers and programme staff with no knowledge of TV have been posted in Doordarshan. As for the post of Director-General, it has always been held by the government that officers of the elite service, the IAS, can handle any job with equal disinterest. The general principles and pattern of AIR also apply to Doordarshan. Where the organisation of Doordarshan differs significantly, the procedure in that department will be separately explained.

The mass media is expected to play an important role in the developmental process, and AIR and Doordarshan therefore maintain close contact with the various governmental and other agencies to achieve this end. These include such Ministries and Departments as Agriculture and Extension, Irrigation, Meteorology, Education, Health and Family Welfare and so on. AIR and Doordarshan have come forward at some time or other to bring to the notice of the public the work of all departments, not excluding the Department of Archaeology which may need public cooperation for the preservation of monuments.

At the centre, contact with Ministries and Departments is maintained on important or major policy issues by the Directors-General. Liaison on matters of lesser importance and follow-up action are carried out by the radio and TV Centres in Delhi. The Director, External Services Division, keeps in touch with the Ministry of External Affairs for guidance and information on foreign policy issues.

In the states it is the function of the regional Station Directors at the state capitals to maintain contact with the government departments and to provide radio and TV support (where TV centres exist) to developmental activities in the region. Generally speaking, a slot in the programme schedule, once a week or once a fortnight, is reserved for state publicity programmes which are fixed up through the state Directors of Information. While it is emphasised that broadcasting stations exist to provide a service for people residing within their service range and no distinction is made between union and state government activities, all attempts at control at the state level have been stoutly resisted.

Finance for Broadcasting

Broadcasting is wholly financed from the Consolidated Fund of India. According to the financial procedure followed under the Constitution, all revenues received, loans raised and money received in payment of loans by the union government go to form the Consolidated Fund. Thus if a department of the government earns revenues, these earnings are credited to the Consolidated Fund and are not retained by the department itself. There are however departments of government which are designated 'commercial departments,' and for such departments a profit and loss account is maintained. The revenues earned by a commercial department are shown in the profit and loss account as the earnings of the department. All India Radio and Doordarshan are included among the commercial departments but this is a book entry and the earnings actually go to the Consolidated Fund. No money can be withdrawn from the Consolidated Fund without an Act of Parliament. The budget of each department is drawn up and included in the Finance Bill for each financial year. It is presented to Parliament by the Finance Minister on 28 February for the new financial year beginning in April. The budget of each department is separately discussed and voted.

The only exception to this procedure is the Indian Railways which is the largest department in the Government of India. The Railways have their own budget which is presented to Parliament separately by the Minister in charge of the Railway budget, a few days in advance of the presentation of the General Budget· The Railways make an annual contribution to the Consolidated Fund.

The budget for AIR and Doordarshan is presented as part of the expenditure of the Ministry of Information and Broadcasting. In accordance with the procedure laid down by government for Ministries and Departments, the budget is divided into two main parts. There is the annual expenditure both on revenue and capital account which is described as non-Plan. The other part refers to Plan, or developmental expenditure. Before a Five Year Plan is due, each department proposes an expansion in terms of defined objectives within the expected financial availability. In these proposals the outlay for each year of the Plan has to be shown separately from the total outlay and accounted for in detail. The draft Plan is scrutinised at various departmental, ministerial and inter-ministerial committees before submission to the Planning Commission which then approves as it thinks fit. Each year within the Five Year period the Plan for the year is scrutinised again, first by the Planning Commission and then by the Ministry of Finance, before the plan expenditure for the fiscal year is accepted and voted by Parliament.

This system of funding, unlike the arrangements in many other broadcasting organisations, operates also for the External Services Division of AIR which receives no funds from the Ministry of External Affairs or any other source. Its system of accounting is precisely the same as that of any other service within the AIR department.

Financial accountability is provided through the Auditor-General of India who audits the Accounts which are placed before Parliament. The Public Accounts Committee of Parliament examines the Accounts and reports directly to the House. In AIR and Doordarshan the Deputy Director-General (Inspection) conducts an internal audit and is charged with responsibility for ensuring that the objections and comments made by the Auditor General and the Public Accounts Committee are expeditiously attended to.

Government maintains a tight control of the expenditures of AIR and Doordarshan and the powers of the Directors-General and of all heads of departments for re-appropriating funds from one head of account to another are strictly limited.

Within the total outlay, Plan and non-Plan, the allocation for each station, the News Services Division, the External Services Division and every other office is separately indicated and within these allocations there are specified heads of accounts. Heads of offices have delegated financial and administrative powers under each head of account and can act independently within these limits. For expenditure over and above these limits the Director-General's approval becomes necessary. For example, Station Directors can pay any one artist or performer a fee up to one thousand rupees and a writer or composer three thousand rupees on account of royalty in any one month. For payments in excess of these amounts the Director-General's permission becomes necessary.

The powers of the Directors-General are themselves limited. As heads of departments they have substantial powers, to incur expenditure on the purchase of machinery, to make appointments etc., as do other heads of departments in the Government of India. But powers which are specially necessary for them in their particular fields are denied them. For example, they cannot send news correspondents by air to cover events if the correspondent does not have the official status to do so. And very few correspondents, if any, are in the salary grade which entitles them to air travel. Directors-General cannot revise the grades of payment to artists, writers and performers which were last revised about fifteen years ago, and so on and so forth. These limitations largely explain why programme expenditure is such a low percentage of the total budgets of AIR and Doordarshan — around 12 per cent and 8.7 per cent respectively. (In this calculation the budget heads taken into account are fees to Staff Artists, Programme Services and Royalties). It also goes a long way in explaining the poor quality of programmes. The inadequacy of funds has been a continuing constraint over the years.

When AIR's Vividh Bharati was commercialised in 1967, as recommended by the Chanda Committee, the object was to augment the financial resources of broadcasting. The Cabinet order which approved the Commercial Service expressly stated that the income derived from commercials should be ploughed back into AIR for improvement of the service through experiments in programming and technology. But the order of the Cabinet was not implemented by the Ministry of Finance for several years. Eventually the matter was taken up by the Ministry of Information and Broadcasting with the Cabinet in 1974. The government's decision was that the 'incremental revenue' from commercials should be handed over to AIR for improvement of programmes. However the matter did not end at this. There followed a protracted argument on the interpretation of the words 'incremental revenue' words used by Indira Gandhi in her noting on the file. AIR and the Ministry of I and B contended that 1974, the year in which the decision was taken, should be treated as the base year, and that all earnings from commercials above the income of that year should be ploughed back into broadcasting. The Ministry of Finance took the view that 'incremental revenue' had to be taken as the increase of revenue of one year over the preceding year. Thus, if in 1974 commercials had yielded forty-five million and in 1975 fifty million, the 'incremental revenue' would amount to only five million and so on from year to year. This issue was eventually resolved in 1976 with the setting up of the AIR and Doordarshan (Commercial Services Revenue) Non-Lapsable Fund (NLF) and the adoption of 1975 as the base year. The opening balance for AIR and Doordarshan was Rs.11,540,000. Doordarshan started accepting commercial spots in January 1976, and sponsored programmes such as Soap opera serials started in 1983. Rates of commercials have been revised approximately once in five years.

The government order establishing the Fund was issued in February 1977 and made retrospective from November 1976. The Non-Lapsable Fund (NLF) was formed out of the revenues earned out of Commercial Services of AIR and Doordarshan after deducting commission paid to agents and discount to advertisers. The actual net revenue is transferred to the Fund each year and appears in the budget as 'Contribution to the Akashvani (AIR) and Doordarshan Non-Lapsable Fund'.

The Fund is operated by a board consisting of representatives of the Ministries of Information and Broadcasting, Finance, the Department of Electronics, the Planning Commission and the Directors-General of AIR and Doordarshan. Each year a sum of money from the NLF is included in the budgets of the two Departments. They are required to prepare schemes showing how the money is proposed to be spent and how it will result in the improvement of programmes. The schemes have to be placed before the Board for approval.

A clear-cut-policy has yet to emerge as to how the NLF monies are to be spent. The representatives of the Ministry of Finance and the Planning Commission have been openly hostile. Their argument is that in the final analysis all monies come from a common kitty. If AIR and Doordarshan are getting funds from the NLF they can do with that much less in their annual budgets and a proportionately smaller share of Plan funds. That their argument has prevailed is evident from the manner in which the rules of the NLF were revised in 1981 and again in 1983. Four important modifications took place. First, expenditure under the head Programme Services for all stations is met from the NLF. It is from this head that performers of all categories, advisers and consultants are paid. It accounts for approximately 5 per cent of the budget of AIR and Doordarshan.

Second, the entire expenditure of the Commercial Services of AIR and Doordarshan is debited to the Fund.

Third, an annual grant is made to the TV Wing of the Film and Television Institute of India, Pune, an autonomous body which functions under the Ministry of I. & B., to improve its soft and hardware facilities. On an average the institute runs two in-service training courses a year for Doordarshan staff.

Fourth, an annual grant is made to the Indian Institute of Mass Communication in New Dehi, which enjoys a status similar to that of the Pune Institute. This organisation provides training in the print medium, audio-visual advertising and radio and TV. Staff in AIR and Doordarshan's News and Current Affairs Sections are trained here. The training is almost entirely in the form of lectures since the Institute has hardly any equipment which the students can operate to acquire skills in radio and TV production.

In short, what the government has given with one hand, it has taken back with the other. A substantial part of the funds intended for the improvement of programmes is being used to pay for routine services which the government was previously providing. Several software schemes previously financed from Plan funds were in the Sixth Plan shifted to the NLF.

Funds for programmes remain at the abysmally poor level where they were before the NLF came into existence. Over the past five years the monies spent on programme services have gone up by approximately three million rupees annually that is, by 12 per cent. The total budget has increased by 13 per cent. In the case of Doordarshan, programme expenditure has risen by approximately four million rupees annually (excluding the first of the five years under consideration when it went up by only two million). During the period as a whole Doordarshan's revenue budget more than trebled itself but the programme expenditure merely doubled itself. The figures tell their own tale of the low priority given to software in Doordarshan, particularly considering that the net revenue from commercials rose to three times its former level. It would be useful to look at some basic figures in the budget grants of the two Departments over the past five years. (See Table 3.1)

It has been the declared policy of the government ever since the First Plan that public cooperation in the developmental process is essential and this implies that the people should be informed of what is being done to improve their lot and what they themselves can do to utilise the opportunities offered. The mass media therefore, is seminal to the entire business of development. The facts, however, tell a different story as the comparative figures of the percentage of outlays to three departments during the Five Year Plans indicate (see Table 3.2).

Table 3.1

Budget Grants to AIR and Doordarshan
(in million rupees)

	AIR				DOORDARSHAN			
	Plan	Non-Plan	Total	Net Commercial Revenue	Plan	Non-Plan	Total	Net Commercial Revenue
1980-81 Revenue	21	509	530	110	24	206	231	81
Capital								
1981-82 Revenue	14	593	607	129	29	269	298	115
Capital			198				136	
1982-83 Revenue	18	631	649	133	35	388	425	159
Capital			256				360	
1983-84 Revenue	24	698	722	158	46	433	479	198
Capital			330				579	
1984-85 Revenue	37	778	815	104	95	616	711	260
Capital			528				719	

Note: Figures have been rounded to the nearest whole number.
Source: Ministry of Information and Broadcasting, *Annual Reports to Parliament.*

Table 3.2

Outlays to Three Departments (Percentages)

Years	Plan	Broadcasting	Telecommunications	Education
1951-56	First	0.2 %	2.2 %	7.0 %
1956-61	Second	0.2 %	1.3 %	6.4 %
1961-66	Third	0.19%	1.15%	7.5 %
1969-74	Fourth	0.25%	1.35%	7.6 %
1974-79	Fifth	0.23%	3.2 %	3.27%
1979-84	Sixth	0.22%		2.6 %
1984-89	Seventh	0.77%	2.15%	3.5 %

Source: Plan documents.

The Organisation of Planning and Development

We have discussed the question of finance provided for the development of broadcasting. It would be worthwhile to look into the organisational arrangements in the two directorates for this purpose. When planning first started in AIR with what is known as the Pilot Project in 1947, a post of Deputy Director-General (Planning) was created. It was held by S. Gopalan, an engineer by profession who had subsequently come over to the programme side. He was well-equipped to preside over AIR's development and to coordinate its programme and technical aspects. After his departure the post was surrendered, and the Directorate-General accepted a lower post, that of Director of Programmes (Planning). The actual duties assigned to this officer had nothing to do with planning. He looked after contractual matters, chiefly Staff Artists' contracts! The result was that planning became the responsibility of the Planning and Development Unit (Engineering) under the Engineer-in-Chief. This Unit located areas not served by existing transmitters and filled the gaps. Studios were conceived of on three standardised designs, type III with the largest number of studios and ample equipment, type II, a smaller number of studios and less equipment, and type I at the bottom of the ladder. What was to be put on the air was thought of afterwards!

The system of forward planning with engineers in charge has been rightly described as putting the cart before the horse. The linguistic composition of the audience and their multifarious needs should be ascertained in the first instance and appropriate technology provided to meet these requirements. In the early sixties, AIR's demands for a full-fledged programme unit was conceded by the Ministry in a niggardly fashion. The Chanda Committee (of which more later) commenting on this situation noted:

> Without programme objectives to guide, its [the Development Unit's] planning was tending to be in a vacuum. Often enough, this did not give flexibility to programme planners who had to be content to plan on the basis of facilities made available rather than on what the station was intended to do. Only recently a Director of Programmes has been appointed but he has not been made a part of the Unit. Advice to be useful should come from within rather than outside. (Chapter III Para 121).

The Programme Planning Unit was strengthened in the early seventies but an Integrated Planning Unit, headed by a senior programme officer has not come into being. Doordarshan has learnt nothing from AIR's experience. It does not have Programme Planning Unit.

A basic lacuna in AIR's system of planning was the total absence of provision for software. Till the Fifth Plan no money was set aside for improving the quality of the programmes, such as engaging more news correspondents, appointing of qualified producers for science and rural programmes and so on. In that Plan a number of software schemes were prepared due to the initiative of the I & B Secretary, A.J. Kidwai, and finally approved, apart from those mentioned. These included the setting up of a national orchestra in Madras on the pattern of the orchestra in Delhi, choral groups at a number of stations to popularise group singing especially among school-children, and to send Indian staff in the External Services to visit the target areas to refresh their knowledge of foreign languages. For Doordarshan, which was still part of AIR, the software schemes included funds for commissioning special TV films by distinguished directors, for drama, documentaries and so forth. Incidentally it was the first time that a separate plan for the development of Doordarshan was drawn up.

It was contended by the Chanda Committee that the projection of five years for planning in television is unsatisfactory; projections should be for twenty years. This does not seem to me to be valid. A twenty-year projection could at best formulate broad objectives and would have to be broken down into shorter time spans with targets set and concrete steps spelt out for achieving the more immediate goals. The basic defects of our system of planning seem to be the following: First, rigidity: quite a few schemes approved in one Plan are carried over to the next Plan, due to delays of one kind or another. However, modification of schemes is not really possible. If you wish to modify, you have to abandon the old scheme and start afresh — and there is no guarantee that the new scheme will be accepted. So rather than risk a total loss AIR has frequently implemented a scheme which it knew to be defective. Second, the government's system of planning leaves little room for accommodating changes in technology, because of this rigidity. Third, the emphasis in planning is on new schemes, no doubt to gain political kudos. Little is done to consolidate and improve schemes already in existence. Fourth, when a new Plan is being formulated, there is little or no indication of the monies likely to be available for each department. Ministries, in the hope of getting more if they ask for more, jack up their proposals in a wild and extravagant manner. For example, in the Fifth Plan the proposals formulated by AIR and Doordarshan amounted to five thousand million rupees; what was sanctioned was just over one-fifth of this! Imagine the waste of effort involved, time and effort which could have been usefully spent on practical steps to improve efficiency. The Finance Secretary deserves sympathy; growing demands of the ministries on the one hand and instructions of the cabinet not to exceed the approved allocations on the other. At a meeting of the Planning Commission to discuss AIR's Plan allocations at which this author was present, he turned to the Ministry's Financial Adviser and said, 'You know what to do. Don't reply for the first six months and then tell them the file is lost.' The advice was unnecessary as the Financial Adviser was already doing this.

Planning, as we have seen, has been largely a matter of putting up transmitters to fill gaps in coverage, to improve studio facilities. Initially there were improvised studios in rented buildings, thereafter regular studios, and finally since 1971 a little titbit for programmes. Sometimes the first objective and sometimes the second have been given priority in the Five Year Plans. However, special mention should be made of the Third Plan, otherwise known as the Medium-Wave Plan, which came into operation in 1961. A number of rebroadcast centres were set up, which consisted of a medium to high power transmitter to which a single multi-purpose studio was attached. These centres were designated Auxiliary Centres and were located several miles outside cities. Programmes prerecorded at the station at the state capital were passed on and transmitted by the Auxiliary Centre so that they could be available to the outlying areas of each state on cheap medium-wave receivers. Subsequent plans have sought to develop Auxiliary Centres into full-fledged radio stations. This has necessitated building studios in the city where they are easily accessible to artists and talkers. In the Plan documents, studio projects were referred to as Auxiliary studios. In just a few cases, studios were provided in district towns because of their cultural importance. But there was no transmitter. Programmes recorded at Auxiliary studios were transmitted by the station located at the state capital. In such cases the intention has been to establish an 'Auxiliary transmitter' for each Auxiliary studio. This process of making Auxiliary Centres and Auxiliary studios into full-fledged stations is now all but complete. To understand the legend of the map of AIR stations (see p. 72) these facts have to be kept in mind.

All India Radio

Radio Services

AIR operates 167 medium- and short-wave transmitters. This includes five FM transmitters which cover approximately 90 per cent of the population. Eighty-seven radio stations carry zonal, and regional services in Hindi, English and regional languages. So far there is only one 'local' station with an FM transmitter. Four Yuv Vani channels of programmes for young people broadcast between 4.5 and 6 hours a day.

The News Services Division, NSD, operates with 34 Regional News Units and transmits 68 national news bulletins a day in nineteen languages and 124 Regional bulletins in 64 languages and dialects in the Home Services. There is a Commercial Service which functions from 29 stations. Commercial spots and sponsored programmes are accepted. The External Services carry 65 news broadcasts a day in twenty-five languages.

AIR also operates a Transcription and Programme Exchange Service and separate Staff Training Institutes for programme and engineering staff. Four Regional Engineering Offices are responsible for developmental projects and equipment maintenance in their respective areas.

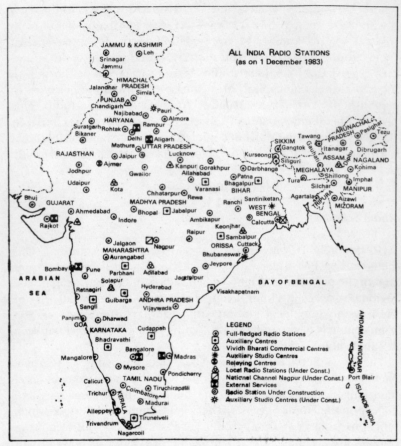

All India Radio Stations (as on 1 December 1983)

LEGEND

⊙ Full-fledged Radio Stations
⊡ Auxiliary Centres
△ Vividh Bharati Commercial Centres
▲ Auxiliary Studio Centres
○ Relaying Centres
■ Local Radio Stations (Under Const.)
◧ National Channel Nagpur (Under Const.)
✕ External Services
⊘ Radio Station Under Construction
✳ Auxiliary Studio Centres (Under Const.)

Source: Ministry of Information and Broadcasting, Report to Paliament, 1983-84, p. 19.

Based on Survey of India outline map.

Directorate

The senior officer in the Directorate-General of AIR next to the Director-General is the Engineer-in-Chief who is head of the technical services. The Director-General is also assisted by six Deputy Directors-General located in Delhi of whom five are responsible respectively for Programmes, the Commercial Service, Internal Inspection, Administration and Security. The Director of the News Services Division is ex-officio Deputy Director-General but in practice he reports to the Deputy Director-General (Programmes) on routine matters and directly to the Director-General on important issues. The DDG (Administration) is an officer of the Central Government's administrative services seconded to hold this post for a limited tenure, and the DDG (Security) is a police officer of the rank of a Deputy Inspector-General of Police. All the other DDGs belong to AIR's regular programme cadre.

There are three posts of Deputy Director-General for the regions. They are located at Calcutta, Gauhati and Bombay. During the last decade the organisation has grown considerably in size and much more detailed work is going into the planning of programme services such as Farm and Home, Education, Family Welfare and Sports. It was considered that there was too much centralisation in AIR and the Directorate-General in Delhi could not efficiently control a network which had proliferated as widely as AIR. The creation in 1976 of two posts of DDG in Calcutta and Bombay and of the third subsequently has slightly eased the pressure at Delhi. The offices of the Regional Deputy Directors-General are inadequately staffed and they are therefore not in a position to shoulder the responsibilities intended.

Below the DDGs come a number of Directors of Programmes, Directors of Farm and Home, Family Welfare, the Director of Audience Research and Chief Producers for Music, Drama, Features and Educational programmes who are specialists in their fields. Mention should be made of a unit which is concerned with forward software planning in terms of the needs of audiences. It is responsible for the preparation of the detailed draft plans, annual and five yearly, which are submitted to government and the Planning Commission. Interestingly enough, this unit came into existence in the early sixties and for a good ten years accomplished little. Planning in AIR has been an engineering affair, with transmitters taking first priority, studios coming next and software a poor third. This story has been repeated in Doordarshan, especially since 1983 when the government undertook its plan for rapid expansion adding no less than 126 transmitters in one year but not a single studio, and of course no provision for software.

The Programme Division is responsible for the supervision of the programme schedules of AIR stations, for on-the-spot study of the working of their programme sections and for the issue of directives and monitoring. The division maintains contact with departments of government and unofficial agencies and is responsible for the preparation of briefs for Parliamentary committees and drafts for the Minister's replies to the numerous questions raised in Parliament. Finally it is responsible for the planning, production and publicity of national or network programmes which constitute approximately 5 per cent of AIR's output.

The DDG in charge of the Commercial Service is located in Delhi but the major work of selling time, approving commercial spots and sponsored programmes and maintaining contact with the advertising agencies is carried out by the Central Sales Unit under the charge of a senior Director in Bombay because of its importance as a commercial centre.

The Internal Inspectorate is a special unit of programme, administrative and accounts staff, set up in the early fifties to inspect the stations and offices of AIR. In addition to the regular audit of accounts, the administrative procedures and problems of the station are examined. Most important, there is a 'performance audit' of programmes and the DDG and his team are expected personally to examine the station's relations with the state government, public bodies and the press. All complaints are enquired into.

In AIR the technical services, transmitters, studios and receiving centres, function under the Engineer-in-Chief (E-in-C). He is assisted in the Directorate-General by several Chief Engineers. This rank is equal to that of DDG. One of these officers is responsible for maintenance and another for development.

On the engineering side, AIR is divided into four regions, each of which is placed under a Regional Engineer who is of the rank of a Superintending Engineer. New projects within the region and maintenance of studios, transmitters and receiving centres are the responsibility of the Regional Engineer. Inspection of stations on the technical side is also one of the functions of the Regional Engineer.

An important branch of the engineering division is the Directorate of Frequency Assignments. This branch works under a senior engineer and is responsible for allocating the frequencies of AIR transmitters, coordinating the use of transmitters for news and other services and supervising their accuracy through a number of monitoring centres set up in different parts of the country. A Chief Engineer (Civil Construction Wing) is on secondment to AIR, heads the Civil Wing and is responsible for the construction and maintenance of buildings of both AIR and Doordarshan.

The DG's Chief Assistant for administration is the DDG (Administration) who is also his internal financial adviser. He is assisted by a Director of Finance and Administration, several deputies and clerical staff. Budget and financial control, all matters relating to personnel welfare and complaints are dealt with in this division.

Zonal, Capital and Regional Stations

The bedrock of the Indian broadcasting system is the radio station which as mentioned above produces, mainly in its regional language or languages, 70 per cent of the programmes radiated from its transmitters. AIR radio stations fall into three classes, zonal, regional and local.

The zonal stations are the four stations at Delhi, Calcutta, Madras and Bombay, each broadcasting on two or more channels with short-wave and medium-wave transmitters. Delhi, the central station in the AIR network, serves two purposes. First, it caters to a regional audience on its two channels, known as A and B. The channel A, which is the more powerful, presents programmes and news bulletins in Hindi, the main language of the region. The B channel carries programmes and news in English, Hindi, Urdu and Punjabi, and also broadcasts western music. Indian music in all its varieties is available on both A and B channels. National or network programmes are carried on either A or B channel and additional frequencies are provided to facilitate relay. Delhi also has a Yuv Vani or youth channel which operates for some six and a half hours a day. Thus listeners around Delhi have a choice of four channels, Delhi A and B, the Commercial Service and Yuv Vani.

The A and B and Yuv Vani channels function under the Station Director of the Delhi station. The Commercial Service is headed by its own Station Director who is responsible to the DDG (Commercial).

The Engineer-in-Charge of Broadcasting House in New Delhi is responsible for the functioning of the studios and other facilities which are shared by the News Services Division and the External Services Division.

The other three zonal stations operate on similar lines. Calcutta has four channels, Bombay and Madras have three each with no Yuv Vani channel. But as with most stations which do not at present have separate Yuv Vani channels, Bombay and Madras provide time on their existing channels for youth programmes, planned and presented on the same lines as the Delhi Yuv Vani.

The capital stations are located at the capitals of the different states. Most of them have only one medium-wave channel. A few have two or more; for example, Hyderabad (Andhra Pradesh) has three channels including a Yuv Vani service and Srinagar (Kashmir) and Gauhati (Assam) have two channels each. At most of these stations there are separate Commercial Broadcasting Service centres operating a commercial channel.

A third category is comprised of the broadcasting stations located within the same state as a capital station. Depending on linguistic and cultural factors there is a degree of programme-sharing between the capital station and the regional stations within the state. The capital station is in any case responsible for coordinating broadcasts in support of state development programmes and for liaison with the state government. The regional stations are all single channel stations with the sole exception of Jammu in J&K state which has a Yuv Vani channel.

A fourth category of stations is that constituted by 'local stations.' So far there is only one such station, located in Nagercoil in Tamil Nadu. Five other such local stations were projected in the Sixth Plan but did not come up. The purpose of local stations is to involve the local people in programmes for their own development.

The engineers responsible for the studios, transmitter and receiving centre are part of the Station Director's establishment. A commercial channel is located at each of twenty-nine of these stations, operating under its own director. An AIR station consists of Programme, News and Engineering branches reporting to the Station Director, the head of the station in the vast majority of cases. In a few cases a senior engineer is head of the office.

The Programme Branch is responsible for the planning and production of programmes in accordance with a skeleton chart, which is approved by the AIR Directorate-General. The skeleton chart determines such basic facts as the languages of broadcast and the proportion of the time given to each; relays of central bulletins; the relative time given to music of different kinds; the special audience programmes, as for example rural and tribal programmes, educational broadcasts and so forth. Within this broad framework, the budget and the financial limits of the Station Director's powers under different budget heads, he has in theory almost complete autonomy in programme matters. Programmes are planned quarterly and the station is required to send copies to the Directorate-General for information. These schedules are examined by the relevant sections and Directors of Programmes, Chief Producers and Deputy Chief Producers at headquarters who send such comments as they think fit for the consideration of the Station Director. As already mentioned, the Deputy Director-General (Inspection) and his team visit stations periodically for a thorough audit of all aspects of the station's functioning. The regional Deputy Director-General and other senior officers also visit stations to examine and advise on particular programme activities.

The Station Director (SD) is assisted by one or more Assistant Station Directors (ASD). Under the ASD work the various Programme Branches, such as music, drama, talks and discussions, rural programmes, educational broadcasts and so on. These programmes are planned and produced by two categories of staff, Programme Executives and Producers. The PEXs are regular government servants while the Producers, script-writers, announcers are Staff Artists on contract. Incidentally, the largest category of Staff Artists at a radio station consists of musicians, that is instrumentalists and a few composers. With a few exceptions, when a singer or a sitar player comes to perform, the accompanists, such as a tabla player, tanpura and sarangi players or whoever else is necessary is provided by the station. Many of the musicians on the staff, veena, sitar and tabla players and flautists have been among the top-ranking musicians of the country.

Thirty-four stations have Regional News Units under the administrative control of the Station Director but reporting professionally to the Director of the News Services Division in Delhi. This dual control occasionally creates problems since the local authorities, and the public for that matter, hold the Station Director responsible for whatever emanates from the station and are not aware of, or concerned with, the internal procedures of AIR.

The Station Director has an Administrative Officer to deal with finance, staff management and other administrative work. Sixteen AIR Stations have Audience Research Units, with an Audience Research Officer on the Station Director's staff who is responsible professionally to the Director, Audience Research, in Delhi.

The Station Engineer, even if he is junior to the SD and is under his administrative control, is autonomous and decides all engineering matters and controls the Engineering budget heads and the Engineering staff. Relations between Engineers and programme staff have been a serious problem since the seventies. 'Functional freedom' is the great slogan. Often there is little team spirit, and as a result the output can be of poor quality.

News Services

The News Services Division functions under a Director (DNS) who is an ex-officio Deputy Director-General. In the central office in New Delhi the DNS is assisted by several deputies, one Chief News Editor and reporting staff of various categories, senior correspondents, and reporters, responsible for the professional work of the NSD. Studios and technical facilities in Delhi are shared between the Delhi Station, the News Services Division and the External Services.

The administrative wing of the DNS's office is organised along the lines of similar branches at AIR stations. The professional staff in the NSD fall into two broad categories: staff artists (such as news readers, translators, language sub-editors in the Indian Language Units), and officers of the Central Information Service (CIS). The Director, his deputies and all the senior editorial and reporting staff belong to this service.

As already mentioned there are in addition to the Central office, Regional News Units at thirty-four AIR stations. These Units function under a News Editor and one or two senior staff members drawn from the CIS. Others such as news translators and readers are staff artists.

The creation of the CIS has had its own repercussions. CIS officers are jacks-of-all-trades. A CIS officer may be doing editorial work in the Publications Division and may be well qualified as a manager in book production. He may have no experience of, and little interest in, news reporting in AIR which would well be his next assignment. In the last decade several CIS officers who had little or no journalistic experience and had not served in this department earlier in their careers have been appointed Directors of the News Services Division. Specialisation in radio journalism is at a discount in the NSD.

The creation of the CIS has had an even more serious and damaging effect on the news and current affairs output of AIR. Apart from AIR the other departments of the Ministry exist specifically to publicise the government. AIR's NSD is basically a news organisation with far wider objectives than government publicity. Persons brought up to function as publicity agents of the government may not be in a position in a short tenure with AIR to appreciate or absorb the aims and objectives of a public service broadcasting organisation. These are some of the issues which have been raised by the two review committees which have examined the working of AIR — the Chanda Committee (1964) and the Verghese Working Group (1977).

External Services

The External Services Division (ESD) resembles in organisation an AIR station, but where in a station the programme units are divided by subjects, for example music, talks and discussions, drama and features, the ESD programme units are based on language. The largest and the most important groups are the English and Urdu services which are on the air daily for some ten and a half and twelve and a half hours respectively. Among other units for the twenty-five languages of the services are the Chinese, Indonesian, Burmese, Pushto and Persian services.

The Director of ESD is a Station Director in the senior scale assisted by Deputy Directors and junior staff. The Programme staff are responsible for planning and organisational work. Each foreign language unit is under a Supervisor who is a specialist in the language. Only Indian nationals are eligible for appointment as Supervisors. The work of translation and presentation is performed by translator-announcers who may be Indians or foreigners and most units include both. Supervisors and translator-announcers are both Staff Artists. News bulletins for the various External Services programmes are provided in English by the NSD and translated by the language units. There is a Special Talks Unit in ESD of CIS officers who prepare news commentaries and reviews of the Indian press for the different services.

Transcription and Programme Exchange Service

The Transcription and Programme Exchange Service was set up as a separate office in Delhi in the early fifties. It functions under a Director (DTPES) who is of the rank of an SD and is assisted by programme and technical staff. All AIR stations are required to send to the DTPES recordings of music, talks, plays, features and other programmes which are of high quality and may be of interest to wider audiences than those commanded by the originating stations, and to supply scripts in Hindi, English and Urdu. The TPES issues a fortnightly bulletin to all stations listing the programmes available with short descriptive notes, from which the stations can choose items for re-broadcast. Royalty and other re-broadcast fees, in accordance with the terms of the original programme contract, are payable by the stations which re-broadcast the programme.

The use of Programme Exchange Service material varies considerably from station to station depending mainly on two factors, the station's own resources for programmes of a particular type, and language. For example, some of the smaller stations do not have much talent for classical music within their own region, and therefore make considerable use of tape recordings of the foremost artists. All stations make some use of recordings of artists from other areas. In a large number of stations the main language of broadcast is Hindi and there is a considerable use of the spoken word programmes in Hindi offered by the service; and to a lesser extent this applies also to available English and Urdu programmes. However, the maximum use of transcription material is in respect of music.

The office of the Director, Transcription and Programme Exchange Service also houses the AIR Archives which currently consist of 26,700 tapes, scripts, other written material and photographs of great historical value. Recordings of the views of national figures such as Mahatma Gandhi, Rabindra Nath Tagore, Jawahar Lal Nehru, Sardar Vallabhbhai Patel, Netaji Subhas Chandra Bose, and of Lord Mountbatten are available. Recordings by distinguished musicians and literary figures are also preserved in the archives.

This material is brought before the public from time to time in various ways. Special broadcasts are transmitted on birth anniversaries, such as feature programmes on different aspects of the person's contribution, which include excerpts from voice recordings and other relevant material. AIR has released to the Gramophone Co. of India Ltd (HMV) recordings of the prayer speeches of Mahatma Gandhi which are available for sale in the market. Selected recordings of speeches of Jawahar Lal Nehru, Indira Gandhi and a few other national leaders have similarly been released. In the case of musicians AIR has released over fifty recitals by old masters to various gramophone companies, who have reproduced them on commercial discs available in the market. The companies are required to credit AIR, both on the disc and on the sleeve, and to pay royalties directly to the artists or their heirs. Regular periodic national or network music programmes are based on material drawn from the archives, and AIR stations can indent material from the archives for use in their own programmes.

There is no general system of public access to the archives. In a few cases when scholars have asked to listen to recordings for research purposes, arrangements have been made for play-back under supervision.

A museum collection of old technical equipment of archival interest such as transmitters, and recording machines, is maintained in a section of the office of the Research Engineer.

Doordarshan

Television Services

Doordarshan consists of ten full-fledged kendras. (The word kendra means centre and is common to several Indian languages. It is usual to speak of stations in the case of radio and of kendras in the case of TV). The kendras are Delhi, Bombay, Calcutta, Madras, Srinagar, Lucknow, Jalandhar, Bangalore, Trivandrum and Guwahati. Two of these, Delhi and Bombay, have two channels, started in September 1984 and May 1985 respectively. The last three mentioned hardly qualify as centres since they are not yet in a position to originate programmes. They should do so in a short while. The establishment of kendras in state capitals is a high priority in the Seventh Plan.

There are ten post-SITE Centres which transmit programmes for rural audiences. Seven of these came up shortly after SITE — Jaipur, Raipur, Muzzaffarpur, Gulbarga, Hyderabad, Sambalpur and Pij-Ahmedabad. Three came up later, at Nagpur, Rajkot and Gorakhpur.

A SITE continuity centre is primarily a transmitting centre and functions under a Station Engineer. A film camera team of camera-men and producers is provided at each centre for local coverage. This material is sent back to the Base Production Centre for processing and inclusion in the video packages which are broadcast from each centre.

A Base Production Centre functions under a Station Director and has a full complement of programme and technical staff for the studio. They assemble the complete packages on one-inch tape for each SITE continuity centre and send it on for transmission. There are three Base Production Centres, as there were during SITE, located at Delhi, Hyderabad and Cuttack.

The centre at Ahmedabad-Pij needs a word of explanation. Gujarat was not one of the states included in SITE. Ahmedabad, the capital of this state, is the headquarters of ISRO who were responsible for the up-links, the entire technical ground arrangements, for evaluation and also for the production of some science programmes for SITE in 1975-76. In the circumstances it was considered unfortunate for Ahmedabad to be left out of SITE. ISRO already had an experimental studio in Ahmedabad and it was able to procure a 1-kilowatt transmitter which was set up in Pij, a rural area about 40 kms from Ahmedabad. SITE programmes were transmitted from the Ahmedabad-Pij centre and some additional programmes were also broadcast. This centre was provided with a 10-kilowatt transmitter in November 1983 and provides a service for a million persons.

There are 156 high- and low-power transmitters which relay the regional programmes of the main kendra if it happens to be telecast in the same regional language. The National Programmes are relayed on all transmitters and for the majority of viewers this is the only programme available to them. INSAT I B provides the link for the national relay. The network makes programmes available to 52 per cent of the population. Schemes now under way, especially in the north-eastern states will shortly extend the coverage to 80 per cent of the population.

News bulletins are telecast four times in the network programme every evening. Two of these are of twenty minutes duration, one each in Hindi and English. Two headline bulletins come at the close of the transmission. All the main kendras telecast their own news in their respective regional languages. These languages are Hindi, Bengali, Kashmiri, Marathi, Tamil, Telugu, Kannada, Punjabi, Urdu and Gujarati. The Trivandrum kendra also produces its own news in Malayalam.

The Commercial Service of Doordarshan started functioning in January 1976. What this really means is that Doordarshan has gone commercial. In the beginning only spots were accepted and the total duration given to spots is not supposed to exceed 10 per cent of the transmission time. Since 1983, however, sponsored programmes are also being accepted in greater and greater measure. A Programme Exchange Service has been functioning for several years for the exchange of programmes between the kendras. This was specially necessary before the network programmes became possible. It confined its services to internal circulation. More recently, the exchange service has been engaged in sending programmes on artistic and cultural subjects to a large number of countries with whom India has cultural exchange agreements.

Directorate

Doordarshan's Directorate-General is organised on lines similar to AIR's. Till 1984 the Director-General was one rung lower in the official hierarchy than the DG AIR but since then he has been raised to the same status. The head of the Engineering Division however still ranks one step lower than his counterpart in AIR being only the senior-most Chief Engineer in the service. There are a dozen officers of the same status in the service.

There are three Deputy Directors-General who between them share responsibility for news and current affairs. There is an Additional Director-General of the rank of a Joint Secretary to Government and two Deputy-Directors-General who deal with news and current affairs, planning, the commercial service and inspection. Below them come officers designated Controllers of Programmes, who correspond to Directors in AIR. On the engineering side the Chief Engineer is assisted by Superintending Engineers and others.

There are two sections in the Doordarshan Directorate which do not have counterparts in AIR. These deal with programmes and technical matters connected with the satellite. Programmes prepared at the Base Production Centres to be telecast from the Satellite Centres are supervised and monitored by the programme section while the technical aspects of this operation are the responsibility of the other.

Doordarshan Kendras

Doordarshan kendras are organised on lines similar to AIR stations. Thus programme staff manning the different sections consists of PEX and Staff Artists. There are News Units with CIS staff and staff artists. The significant difference is that the Engineering Staff come under the direct administrative control of the Director. There are no cases in which the head of a kendra is an engineer. However, the SITE-continuity centres which are essentially transmitting units function under an engineer.

Shared Services

When AIR and Doordarshan were separated it was envisaged that certain services would be *shared*. These included Engineering Research, Programme Journals and Audience Research. However after a short while Audience Research was split between the two departments, and Doordarshan now has its own Department of Audience Research though the type of work undertaken and the problems of the two units are similar. With this proviso in mind, Audience Research is being included in this section.

Engineering Research

The activities of the Engineering Research Department are carried out in four sections devoted to propagation, acoustics and audio-engineering, prototype production, and design and development. Some notable work has been done on noise and long-wave propagation, rainfall extenuating margins in the 12 GH band for satellite broadcasting systems, the dynamic range of Indian music and musical instruments and solid state FM link transmitters.

AIR and Doordarshan have a Technical Advisory Committee presided over by a distinguished scientist which includes persons from the National Laboratories and other scientific bodies who are experts in their fields. The function of this committee is to advise AIR/Doordarshan on research and development programmes with reference to work in progress in other research institutions.

Programme Journals

In January 1986 AIR was responsible for publishing eight programme journals in English, Hindi, Urdu, Bengali, Assamese, Tamil, Telugu and Gujarati. These journals had made their appearance at different stages in the development of broadcasting in India. The English language journal, originally called the *Indian Radio Times,* started in 1927, shortly after regular broadcasting commenced under the Indian Broadcasting Company. With the formation of All India Radio, the name of the journal was changed to the *Indian Listener.* In 1956, the name was again changed to *Akashvani. Betar Jagat (Wireless World)*, printed in Bengali, was the first Indian language journal and started publishing in September 1929. The other journals were introduced later. All the language journals were fortnightlies. The English journal was a weekly till a few years ago when it also became a fortnightly. In the early 1950s the circulation of the *Indian Listener* was around 30,000 copies. The highest circulation figure reached by any of the AIR journals was 80,000 copies, achieved by *Betar Jagat* in 1963. It had actually made a profit for three years. At the same time *Vanoli (Tamil)* and *Vani (Telugu)* had circulations of 30,000 and 20,000 respectively. In recent years the journals have not been doing well. Official circulation figures for the last year are pitiful. *Akashvani*'s (English) was the highest at approximately 10,500; *Betar Jagat*'s 6,500; *Vanoli*'s 7,000; *Vani*'s 3,500; and the lowest circulation was that of the Gujarati journal *Nabhovani,* a mere 300.

A Cabinet sub-committee went into the working of the journals and recommended that since they were not financially self-sufficient, and were not likely to become so in the near future, they should be closed down. This happened in early 1986 with three journals, including *Betar Jagat* being wound up in January and the rest following by 31 March. Now, only *Akashvani* (both in Hindi and in English) are published.

In the 1960s India, along with several other Commonwealth countries, had gone into this question of the financial viability of programme journals. The conclusion they reached was that expenditure on journals was a legitimate charge on the programme budgets for publicity and public relations. Journals need not be entirely self-financing. If the principles of financial self-sufficiency were to be applied to AIR journals then it should be applied to other journals. According to my information none of the Government of India's journals is self-financing.

It is true that the journals did not do much to publicise AIR and Doordarshan's programmes. What killed them in the last two decades? The answer is clear: it was the policy of centralisation pursued by the Ministry. The regional language journals were forced to go to Government of India presses even though their charges were higher, the quality of printing was poor and they were continuously late in delivery. All space selling was centralised through the DAVP in Delhi which had neither initiative nor interest. Advertising revenue touched rock bottom. What happened was the logical outcome of a mistaken policy. Moreover, listeners lost interest in the journals since they gave few details about the programmes scheduled for broadcast.

Audience Research

The Audience Research Units function under their respective Directors-General. The units are headed by Directors of Audience Research who are social scientists. They are assisted in AIR by four zonal Deputy Directors at the zonal stations and a fifth is responsible for the Commercial Service. There are twenty-one research units and four mobile units located in different parts of the country. The Audience Research Unit of AIR conducts over 120 field surveys and nearly 1,000 panel surveys during the course of a year. In the field surveys some 44,000 radio and TV households are contacted to assess the quantum of listening/viewing and to determine demographic and other characteristics. Nearly a thousand panel surveys are held in a year and deal with programmes such as music, news and current affairs, drama and festivals. The results are processed on a monthly basis and circulated among programme planners.

Doordarshan has fourteen units attached to its main kendras and post-SITE centres. They attempt to monitor the quantitative viewing of programmes through field surveys, panel surveys, analysis of viewers' letters and the like. Some studies conducted by them have been on subjects such as the impact of TV on children, bench-mark surveys on the family serial *Hum Log* (We People) etc.

The Indian Institute of Mass Communication (IIMC) functions in New Delhi as an autonomous body under the Ministry of Information and Broadcasting. Among other things it conducts studies on the impact of media on audiences. Some of its studies have concerned themselves with AIR/Doordarshan programmes. The two departments cooperate with the IIMC and take note of its findings. Research work has also been conducted by private organisations such as the Operations Research Group (Baroda), the Public Opinion Quarterly and some university departments of communication. All work which impinges on the output of AIR and Doordarshan is seen by senior staff.

A frequent and justified complaint of audience research workers is that little use is made of their findings. In India the explanation for this state of affairs is two-fold. Chiefly, programme planners find themselves up against policy directives which they are in no position to alter. The relay of news bulletins in different languages in AIR provides a case in point. Some single-channel stations broadcast as many as four news bulletins of ten minutes' duration and two each of fifteen minutes between 1800 and 2100 hours. This situation has arisen because government has yielded to pressure groups in Parliament and outside. The result is that there is little of interest for the general listeners. Some of these stations have hardly twenty minutes of music in four of the peak listening hours in the evening and inevitably there have been numerous complaints. Surveys were conducted to listen to news bulletins in Hindi, English and other regional languages in the early 1970s. It was found for instance that there is almost no listening to Hindi news bulletins in Tamil Nadu, Kerala, and Karnataka. Again there was very little listening to English news bulletins in Rajasthan and Bihar except in the capital cities. AIR, therefore, suggested Hindi and English news should not be compulsory relays in the areas where they were not popular and that only one powerful transmitter which could be heard in the state should carry such news. This was the first step towards a sane policy of news relays. The government fought shy of taking a stand on a sensitive issue and after taking the file back and forth for two years decided on sticking to the status quo. And that also because I, then DG, insisted on a decision one way or the other; we had discussed it often enough and there was nothing further to discuss. In the last year or two a similar situation had arisen over the relay of the Hindi news on Doordarshan; the Director had argued as AIR had done earlier but to no effect. Then the Chief Minister of Tamil Nadu threatened dire action if the Madras kendra did not stop the Hindi news relay and this worked. So viewers in Madras are saved this punishment. This is just one example of how audience research is ineffective in the Indian situation.

Audience Research findings for some incomprehensible reason are not open for general circulation, though they are not marked confidential. Summaries of a few of them are published in the newspapers. The result is that the data collected does not help to build up consciousness among the public on the positive and negative effects of programmes.

Staff

Cadres, Contracts and Recruitment

The total number of persons employed in AIR is approximately 16,235 and in Doordarshan 7,980. Of ·these, regular government servants number about 13,879 in AIR and 6,646 in Doordarshan. Staff Artists on contract make up the total.

Regular government servants in AIR and Doordarshan belong to various cadres. These are:

(a) The *Programme Staff cadre*, Programme Executive (PEX), Assistant Station Director (ASD), Station Director (SD), Deputy Director-General (DDG) and Director-General (DG).

(b) The *Engineering Staff cadre*, Assistant Engineer (AE), Assistant Station Engineer (ASE), Station Engineer (SE), Engineer-in-Charge (E-in-c), Deputy Chief Engineer (DCE), Additional Chief Engineer (Ad.CE) and Engineer-in-Chief (E-in-C).

Officers of these cadres have gazetted status and are recruited through the Union Public Service Commission (UPSC). Direct recruitment is mainly at the level of PEX and AE. The posts of Director-General in AIR and Doordarshan are not reserved for officers of the programme cadre. Seven of the thirteen incumbents since Independence up to the end of 1985 have come from this cadre.

In Doordarshan of the five DGS it has had since 1976, the first three were from the joint AIR cadre, while the last two are from the IAS. It is with them that the status of the post has been raised to that of an Additional Secretary to the Government of India.

Promotion to all posts of SD, SE and above are made by departmental promotion committees presided over by a member of the Union Public Service Commission. In each of these cadres there are junior posts for which recruitment is carried out by Selection Boards set up by AIR and Doordarshan along the lines laid down for staff artists.

  (c) *Central Information Service* officers, as already explained, man the higher posts in the news rooms of AIR and Doordarshan.

  (d) *Administrative and Ministerial Staff* drawn from all-India cadres such as the IAS and CSS hold the senior appointments on the managerial side in the two departments. Subordinate staff are recruited on pay-scales and in accordance with procedures which are uniform for all Government of India departments.

  (e) There are other small cadres of posts for specialists, such as Audience Research Officers, Farm Radio Officers etc.

The age of retirement for all regular government servants is 58 years.

Gazetted officers in the Government of India are permitted to form associations but not unions. All other categories of staff may form unions to represent them for rights and privileges. Staff councils exist at various levels to go into staff grievances and representations.

Staff Artists are recruited in accordance with recruitment rules laid down by the Ministry of Information and Broadcasting. Selection boards are convened for different categories of posts. Boards are presided over by the Director-General, a Deputy Director-General, or a Station Director depending on the salary and status of the post which has to be filled. There is a majority of non-officials in a selection board. In the case of the most senior appointments of Staff Artists and for all foreigners the appointing authority is the Ministry. In other cases the appointing authority is the Director-General.

Staff Artists are employed on contract up to the age of fifty-eight. There is a review at this stage and those whose record is satisfactory continue for a further period of two years. Extensions beyond the age of sixty are given only in exceptional cases. Staff Artists enjoy most of the benefits of regular government employees such as housing, medical benefits, leave, travel concessions and the like. Unlike regular government servants they are not entitled to pension, but have the benefit of a contributory provident fund. The lack of opportunities for promotion and the low salaries offered to top class performers are among the basic grievances of Staff Artists.

Training

AIR has had provision for in-service training since 1948. There is a separate institute for Programme and Administrative Training on the one side and another for Technical Training on the other. Both establishments function under the general control of a Deputy Director-General and are part of the office of the Director-General as distinct from separate subordinate offices, such as an AIR station or the News Services Division and the External Services Division. Funds for the institutes are provided within the budget of the Directorate-General.

Two regional training centres have been set up in Shillong in the north-eastern region and in Hyderabad in the south. Between them some sixteen courses were arranged during 1984. General and specialist courses are arranged for different categories of staff which in several cases may mean training in a particular language. The courses, workshops, etc., are planned by the institutes' staff. Senior members of AIR staff and outside experts are invited to lecture, to conduct workshops and demonstrate techniques, and fees are paid to all those invited to lecture or to assist in any way. There is a ceiling on the amount which can be received by a staff member outside the institutes' staff in a financial year. A ten-week course in farm broadcasting was organised by AIR's Staff Training Institute on behalf of the Asian Institute for Broadcast Development (AIBD, Kuala Lumpur), in August-September 1978. Trainees from a dozen Asian countries participated in the course which was the first that AIBD had arranged outside Malaysia. For television, in-service training is provided at the Film and Television Institute of India (FTII) in Pune. The Institute was set up in 1960 initially for film and a television section was added in 1974. While enrolment in the film courses is open to outsiders, only persons already employed in Doordarshan are accepted for training on the television side. Courses at the FTII have varied between six and four months depending on the pressure to open new TV Centres.

Complaints and Redress Procedures

Redress and complaints procedures in broadcasting are the same as for other departments of the Government of India. Every office is required to maintain a complaints box where the public and staff members can drop their complaints. A complaints register is also maintained. Every head of office is required to set aside three hours a week, two hours on one day and one hour on another, when he will make himself available to listen to complaints. Any member of the public or a member of the staff may walk in without appointment to register a complaint with the head of the office. Each office has a Vigilance Officer of appropriate status to take note of and deal with charges of corruption and irregularity.

While complaints and redress procedures look good on paper little seems to be done in regard to public complaints or on those made by staff members. As a result discipline is at a low ebb. The management is supposed to deal only with unions that are duly recognised by the Labour Commissioner. In order to be recognised, several conditions have to be satisfied and the constitution of the union has to be approved. Thereafter, the union has to function in accordance with its own constitution. If, for example, elections are not held as stipulated, the union is de-recognised. In 1984-85 there were few recognised unions in AIR and Doordarshan but numerous unrecognised unions. In fact, the Ministry does deal with the unrecognised unions and forces the DGs to negotiate with them. Office-holders in the unions are able to flout rules of discipline, and disciplinary proceedings against them (time-consuming in any case) come to naught because of political pressure exerted through the Ministry. On the other hand legitimate grievances and demands of the staff, particularly of the badly-paid and insecure staff artists, may not be met for years. The result is that there have been agitations and a few strikes which have been ruthlessly suppressed.

A notable case of this kind occurred shortly before the Asian Games in 1982. Pressure had been building for several years. Staff artists generally, and those in Doordarshan in particular, are badly off in respect of their security of tenure and in the chances of promotion. A body known as the Joint Forum of AIR and Doordarshan, consisting mainly of Staff Artists, had been agitating since 1978 for a 'productivity-linked bonus,' which in effect meant one month's extra salary in each year. Meanwhile, the Posts and Telegraphs Department had granted such a bonus, no doubt because it had a strong union, though the department is notorious for inefficiency and corruption. The Forum threatened to go on strike on 17 November 1982. The government retaliated by taking recourse to the Essential Services Maintenance Act under which strikes in services declared essential are illegal. A large number of well-known Staff Artists were taken into custody. The Forum claimed that over two thousand were arrested. The fact is that radio and TV staff are not, and never have been treated as, Essential Services. If they are to be governed by the disciplinary rules of these services they must also have the concomitant advantages. However, the strike was called off and the staff released. The Minister of Information and Broadcasting in a statement to the press later said that the last time the matter had come up before the Cabinet was in 1980. He admitted that the Forum had a case. (See the *Statesman* and the *Indian Express* of 19 November 1982 and the *Sunday Observer* of 21-27 November 1982.)

On 18 March 1985, the Minister of Information and Broadcasting, replying to questions in the Lok Sabha (the lower house of Parliament) confirmed that there had been some delay in paying salaries to engineering staff at six remote locations where they were putting up transmitters for the grandiose and much publicised 'Special TV Expansion Plan'. He further admitted that no accommodation was available and there was acute shortage of staff.

It is worth pointing out, first that after the salaries were paid, three to six months late, the staff still had to send the money back to their families which meant another delay. (How the families managed without money for three and six months at a time can only be imagined.) Second, regarding accommodation, the fact is that AIR and now Doordarshan, not to speak of the Planning Commission, give the lowest priority to housing. Staff may be sent out to accomplish difficult jobs without a thought about their elementary requirements. Third, concerning staff shortages a small group may be sent out on the understanding that more staff would be sent to help them in the near future. Often, the required complement of staff never arrives.

When radio stations were set up in Jammu and Srinagar in 1948

AIR staff were posted there (described as on tour from Delhi). They invariably received their salaries well after the first day of the month when they were due, sometimes two or three months late. This situation was remedied only after a Station Director was posted and Radio Kashmir staff were integrated into AIR in 1954. At the radio station at Leh in the Ladakh province of Kashmir, situated at a height of 11,500 ft., winter clothing for the staff was not sanctioned for two years. The staff managed because of the help received at a personal level, from the local Army Commander. Incidentally, staff in Leh get less in the way of allowances than their counterparts in Delhi. Their housing compares most unfavourably with that provided to members of the essential services such as the Indo-Tibetan Border Force. It is unlikely that more than a handful of senior officers of the Directorate-General, and not even one from the Ministry has ever visited the border stations at Leh, Tawang (also at about 11,000 ft.), Pasighat and Teju even in the most favourable season. They do not know, and they are not concerned, about the conditions in which the staff have to eke out a miserable existence.

Advisory Bodies and Relations with Outside Institutions

There has been a system of non-official Advisory Committees since the early days of AIR. Membership of successive committees, except for ex-officio members, is in the individual capacity of the person concerned and not as a representative of any group or interest. Rural Advisory Committees, and Tribal and Industrial Programme Advisory Committees at stations where such programmes are originated, function to provide advice and guidance to Station Directors. The most prestigious committees are the Programme Advisory Committees set up to advise on matters of general interest as against the committees which concern themselves with programmes devised for special audiences. Shortly after 1967, when non-Congress governments assumed office in several states, problems abounded concerning the control which state Governments could exercise in the affairs of broadcasting stations in their regions. As a result, the Centre reconstituted the Advisory Committees under the chairmanship of the Minister of State for Information. A few members of the state legislature, including Opposition parties, nominated by the Speaker were represented on the Committees. This procedure did not work and Advisory Committees remained defunct for several years. However, rules have since been framed de-politicising Programme Advisory Committees, and Committees have been reconstituted.

Special attention is paid to maintaining contact with agricultural universities, and in certain cases programmes are produced jointly by stations and universities. There are as many as eight Advisory Committees functioning for the benefit of Doordarshan. These include (1) the Media Advisory Committee at the centre; (2) the Central Advisory Committee for the utilisation of INSAT; (3) Programme Advisory Committees at the Doordarshan kendras; (4) Advisory Committees on various categories of programmes such as family welfare programmes, science programmes and the like.

While broadcasting organisations necessarily maintain contact with a large number of non-official bodies such as academic institutions, social welfare groups etc., such contacts are informal. No official procedure has been laid down for maintaining them.

International Relations

AIR and Doordarshan do not have separate departments for international relations. One officer on the programme side and one engineer in each of the two Directorates-General is appointed as the liaison officer for foreign relations respectively. These officers are responsible for initiating action on such matters as the composition of delegations to represent AIR and Doordarshan at International Conferences, the preparation of briefs and so on.

AIR is a founder-member of the Commonwealth Broadcasting Association (CBA) and of the Asia-Pacific Broadcasting Union (ABU). It has played an active role in the affairs of both. It hosted the General Assembly of the CBA in 1959 and of the ABU in 1968 and in 1978. In 1978-79, as DG, AIR, I was president of ABU. Since its separation from AIR in 1976, Doordarshan has been a member of the CBA and an additional full member of the ABU.

The first Non-Aligned Broadcasting Conference was convened in Sarajevo (Yugoslavia) in October 1977. AIR was a member of a committee which held three preliminary meetings to prepare the draft agenda and other documents for the Conference. The DG AIR was elected as one of the Vice-Presidents and AIR played a major role in drafting the declaration and the action programme issued at the conclusion of the Conference. AIR was elected as a member of the Committee for Cooperation which consists of nineteen members. This Committee functions during the interim period between two meetings of the Non-Aligned Broadcasting Conference. As is well-known, in accordance with the general policy of the non-aligned movement, there is no secretariat of the Conference and the Committee for Cooperation which meets periodically is responsible for implementation of the action programme through the host organisation of the last Conference.

AIR has been a member of the Prix Italia organised by RAI for over two decades and has regularly participated in its annual competitions and has been represented on its juries. AIR was awarded a Prix Italia for its feature programme *Lali and the Lions of Gir* produced by the distinguished Staff Producer Melville de Mellow in 1964.

Apart from the contacts with broadcasting organisations through the Unions and Associations mentioned above, it has been the policy of the Government of India to enter into cultural agreements with other governments. There are some twenty countries with whom cultural agreements have been signed including the Soviet Union, Hungary, Czechoslovakia, Yugoslavia and France. These cultural agreements include a section which deals with broadcasting. Cooperation in the field of technology, exchange of programmes, assistance to visiting news correspondents of other countries, and training and exchange of personnel are included in the agreements. Programme exchange has been largely confined to music but AIR and Doordarshan have also supplied scripts of plays (in English translation) to foreign organisations. In the case of the USA, there is no cultural agreement but there are several joint sub-commissions for cooperation in different fields. The Sub-Commission on Education and Culture has, among others, a committee on radio, television and film. This committee, which on the US side includes representatives of National Public Radio and TV and the private networks, is charged with responsibility for exchanges in the areas just mentioned. In the past few years there have been seminars organised jointly on TV programmes for children, the use of video, etc.

In certain cases, broadcasting organisations have made direct requests to AIR for music, drama recordings and scripts and for other material such as poetry and short stories. Major requests of this kind have come from Mauritius and Fiji where the broadcasting corporations were keen to augment their own resources for Indian music and spoken-word material in Hindi and Urdu. AIR has been supplying such material regularly in large quantities. In all cases of programme exchange AIR is responsible for copyright clearance and royalty payments to authors and performers.

Programme exchanges among members of ABU considered as a group are limited and confined largely to participation in the annual Festival of Asian Music. Substantial exchanges have occurred as already mentioned only in the cases of Fiji and Mauritius which are also members of ABU. Important Muslim and Buddhist festivals in India are given coverage and the programmes are radiated on special frequencies to facilitate relay by two ABU member organisations, Pakistan and Sri Lanka.

In the area of training AIR and Doordarshan have both benefited from and made considerable contributions to the Asian Institute of Broadcast Development (AIBD) in Kuala Lumpur. AIR consistently supported the concept of such an Institute when it was first mooted in ABU, and AIR and Doordarshan have regularly sent programme and technical staff to attend courses at the Institute. They have also deputed staff to function as trainers on particular assignments. In 1982 AIBD organised a special course for TV sports commentators, producers and cameramen in New Delhi to assist Doordarshan to cover the Asian Games. India is among some twenty signatories to the deed sponsoring AIBD and its financial contribution is next only to that of the Government of Malaysia.

It is in the technical field, however, that AIR has played a leading role, and has also benefited from its international contacts in the ABU and in the Non-Aligned Broadcasting Conference. This may be illustrated by the work done in two committees in preparation for the World Administrative Radio Conference (WARC) held in Geneva from September to December 1979. These committees were set up by the Committee for Cooperation of the Non-Aligned Broadcasting Conference. India was represented on both committees. One committee dealt with general issues, the second, of which India was nominated chairman, was concerned with satellites. As a result of the considerable preparatory work done by these committees in 1978-79, the non-aligned countries were able to make common cause on a number of issues vital to them. For example the principle of first-come first-served was rejected for the allocation of frequencies and positions in the geostationary orbit. The interests of developing countries for the allocation of frequencies in the tropical zone were safeguarded and the need for planning and coordinating shortwave frequencies was accepted. The Conference decided to convene a conference to deal with the planning of space services.

In spite of its limited production facilities, Doordarshan has participated in international competitions, mainly in the ABU region and has won numerous awards dating back to 1965. Mention should be made of a documentary which was awarded the TV Prague Prize in 1978 entitled *Alap,* on Ravi Shankar and his music. It was produced by Shukla Das, a young member of Doordarshan Bombay who has since left the service. In 1979 a programme produced by H.R. Salooja of Delhi, *Ray of Hope* was awarded the Prix Futura, EBU.

The Broadcasting System Today:
Objectives, Policies and Programmes 4

Objectives

This chapter indicates the major objectives sought to be achieved through Indian broadcasting, the problems faced and the solutions attempted. It also gives a descriptive account of the chief categories of programmes.

Government and Opposition: Centre and State

In a democratic set-up, all shades of political opinion must have access to radio and TV. This means that (1) Opposition parties must have confidence that their activities are covered in the news and that their viewpoints are adequately represented in current affairs programmes. (2) All recognised parties should have an opportunity to educate the public, according to their lights, on relevant issues, not only at election time but also in the intervening periods. (3) As a corollary to these two points, since 1967 the states have had the right to use AIR and Doordarshan to present their point of view on issues **where they differ from the centre. Until 1967, the Congress party** held sway both at the centre and in the states. If differences arose they were ironed out within the party. Since then governments at the centre and in the states have not been of the same political persuasion and centre-state relations have acquired a new edge. After 1980, there was much talk of redefining centre-state relations to make the constitution 'truly' federal. Control over AIR and Doordarshan is just one of the many bones of contention in this tussle.

News: Government Bias and Suppression

The news departments have faced a good deal of criticism in

Parliament, in the press and in public fora for their collection and presentation of news. Their weaknesses stem from the fact that they are government departments and are bound by rules and procedures in reporting events involving government. Their position is further complicated by the nature of what is taken as news in the Indian situation, although this affects all news media, including the newspapers. These problems are discussed below.

It has been contended in repeated questions in Parliament that Ministers and representatives of the party in power are given disproportionate time in news bulletins which purport to cover debates in the two Houses and public speeches made by MPs and leading political personalities.

Congress and Janata Party Ministers have had to face questions in Parliament on this issue. Their replies have taken the form of counting up the number of lines devoted to reporting the speeches and activities of persons belonging to the major political parties in AIR's news bulletins over a specified period and arguing, on this basis, that time had been reasonably apportioned. They hope to show that, despite being a department of government, AIR reports events objectively and attempts to maintain a balance between the different political parties. (This analysis does not apply to the period of the Emergency when opposition leaders were in prison and there was strict press censorship.) Since Doordarshan news is a replica of AIR news, with the faces of news readers and a few pictures thrown in, a like argument would apply. The principle that the 'dissemination of information, news, and comment should be done in a fair, objective and balanced manner,' and that 'contrasting points of view on events and developments should be presented' has been reiterated in Parliament. On 16 March 1982, the Minister for Information and Broadcasting laid on the table of the upper house a copy of the guidelines issued to his departments to this effect.

The weakness of the procedure of counting lines was exposed by the late U.L. Baruah, who while DG of AIR, addressed a gathering of AIR correspondents in Delhi in 1981. His point was that in reporting the speeches of opposition members AIR news staff picked up inconsequential points but failed to notice the substance of their criticism of the government. This was the core of the opposition's complaint against AIR. He said, "It is not the number of lines [given to reporting the opposition] but it is the substance of it, it is the accuracy, it is the honesty, it is the integrity....' For this he was hauled over the coals. He explained the whole story in an article in the *Statesman* after his retirement, published on 18 April 1983.

Then there is the charge that AIR and Doordarshan suppress uncomfortable facts or at least delay reporting them. In some cases this is wholly due to bureaucratic procedures. On 27 May 1964, Jawaharlal Nehru, Prime Minister of India, suffered a heart attack shortly after 6 AM and lost consciousness, never to recover again. The whole morning AIR said not a word to inform the public that he was hovering between life and death. It simply announced his passing away at 2.25 PM. Over twenty years later, when his daughter Indira Gandhi was assassinated around 9.30 AM on 31 October 1984, AIR did not give out the news until 5.57 PM. Rajiv Gandhi, who was called out of a meeting in West Bengal, and asked to return to Delhi immediately, told the press that he had to tune in to the BBC to find out what had happened to his mother. The story is the same whenever a leading figure dies.

The public blames AIR. They are not aware of an instruction issued by the Government of India, which lays down the procedure to be followed on the death of high dignitaries such as the President, Vice President, Prime Minister and a few others. The news of the death of any of these persons cannot be announced until it has been cleared by the Home Secretary. The AIR correspondent has to get it from him, and inform the News Room, before AIR can broadcast the news. The need for caution is of course evident, as the premature announcement of the passing away of Jaya Prakash Narayan demonstrated. The then Prime Minister, Morarji Desai, was informed in the Lok Sabha on 22 March 1979, probably on the basis of a PTI report from Bombay, that Mr Narayan who was in hospital there had passed away. He announced this to the House which was immediately adjourned. The Prime Minister's announcement and the adjournment of the House was reported by AIR in its news at 1.30 PM without delay. Within minutes the AIR correspondent in Bombay who was at the hospital informed the News Room in New Delhi on the telephone that the news was incorrect and ten minutes after the first announcement AIR was in a position to give correct information. The Prime Minister offered no explanation as to how this error occurred.

In practice all news involving the Government of India, and state governments, and almost any organisation which can count as the establishment, is officially confirmed before it is broadcast by radio and TV. The easiest way for the government to delay or kill an uncomfortable piece of news is to go on delaying the official clearance. Most of the time of AIR correspondents is wasted in government offices trying to clear messages and they get used to official hand-outs instead of going out to observe things for themselves. In the long run, the people are misled and the government itself suffers. Notable examples of misleading reporting of this kind are to be found in the way AIR handled the central government employees' strike in 1960 and the Railway workers' strike of 1973, which practically paralysed the country for several weeks. AIR news picked out for attention insignificant instances in which the strikes had failed. When AIR said trains were running more or less normally, the newspapers published a spate of photographs showing prospective passengers barred from entering the platforms because the gates were closed! If the government wanted public support this was the worst way to go about it. A recent example of delayed reporting, not involving government, is provided by a gas leak which occurred in the northern part of Delhi on the 4 December 1985. The accident took place at about 10.00 AM and thousands of people fled the area and crowded into south Delhi. A senior official of AIR brought the matter to the notice of the News Room. Instead of sending out a correspondent to observe and report, the News Room tried to get an official version from the Delhi Administration. This took them the best part of two hours and AIR came out with its first report and warning to the people of Delhi at 12.30 PM. (See 'Listening Post,' the *Statesman*, New Delhi, 8 December 1985.)

On the fateful morning of 31 October 1984, the BBC reported the news of Mrs Gandhi's assassination at 1.30 and the news soon spread. Mobs were holding up traffic, attacking Sikhs in taxis, scooters and on the streets. Serious arson and looting occurred in several areas of Delhi. AIR did not mention her death until 5.57 PM and there was no mention of the rioting either on AIR or Doordarshan, and hardly any in the days that followed — certainly no pictures of carnage on the screen. Doordarshan extended its transmission round the clock but did little except show endless lines of people 'paying their homage' to Indira Gandhi whose body lay in state at Teen Murti House. Earlier in 1982 a greater tragedy had hit the country in Assam, when Mrs Gandhi insisted on going through an election drawn up on the basis of the 1971 census, against the advice of responsible officers and political parties. Here tribals of different groups, Bengalis and Muslims were caught up in inhuman feuds. The carnage at Nellie was a symbol of the tragedy. In all seven thousand people are believed to have lost their lives in a fortnight. Far removed from the seat of power in Delhi, and with no wealthy international fraternity to get them publicity on the world media which the Sikhs had, Assam was forgotten. Busy with the Asian Games, Doordarshan could not spare one camera team then, or even later, to report what had befallen their brethren in a strategically important part of their country. AIR tucked away the news in a few lines in its news bulletins.

The official defence for delaying, and in some cases totally suppressing, news of rioting is that it triggers off reprisals. It is to guard against reprisals that AIR and Doordarshan and also the Press do not identify the communities involved. An exception was made when Gandhiji was murdered. The announcement said that the assassin was a Hindu.

The position of the official media in reporting riots is indeed delicate. To begin with the public itself demands a far greater degree of accuracy from them than it does from the press. An inaccurate report on AIR or Doordarshan can have serious consequences, and this no doubt is due to the immediacy of these two services. For example, during the elections to the Lok Sabha in March 1977, a mistaken report on the result of one seat in Kashmir resulted in mob violence and the loss of one life, despite the fact that the news was broadcast in only one bulletin and corrected within twenty minutes. On the other hand it is a mistake to suppose that blacking out news from AIR and Doordarshan stops it from gaining currency. The moment something unsavoury is rumoured every one turns to the BBC, Radio Pakistan etc. This happened repeatedly during the Emergency, when there was rigid censorship. It is also important to remember that responsible and full reporting can have a stabilising effect. Candid official reports help to scotch rumours. Unfortunately we have not drawn the correct inference from the announcement about Gandhiji's death. Had the community of the assassin not been named, people would have jumped to the conclusion that he was a Muslim and a carnage of innocent people would have followed. And that mostly is what happens in communal riots now.

A persistent criticism of AIR's news bulletins is that they contain a preponderance of political news to the near exclusion of news of economic and scientific developments, social and cultural events, and even of sport. This criticism is in turn linked with the view that news bulletins are over crowded with statements by Ministers and other dignitaries and contain little hard news. The content analysis of AIR news bulletins undertaken by the Indian Institute of Mass

Communication, Delhi, for three representative fortnights in 1977-78 shows that the complaint is justified to a considerable extent. Items of a political nature occupied 54 per cent of the national news bulletins, and the remainder was divided between fourteen categories which included economic affairs, agriculture, education, science and technology, health, sport and cultural affairs.

On the other hand, it has been argued that in India statements by politicians make news to a far greater extent than in Western countries. The Indian newspapers are dominated by reports of statements made by politicians and AIR is criticised if it omits to mention a statement which is reported in the press. AIR has been taking steps to meet this criticism. As already stated, a daily sports news bulletin in both Hindi and English has been introduced. A daily newsletter of five minutes' duration which covers developmental news is broadcast from Delhi to be relayed by stations; each newsletter is devoted to a different state, and the stations themselves broadcast newsletters which cover developments in their districts. A daily news bulletin of ten minutes' duration has been introduced in Delhi which consists exclusively of what may be described as human interest stories. Science reporters have also been appointed to several AIR stations, especially to report on significant developments in Indian National Laboratories and other pure and applied research centres.

While the paucity of district and local news is a criticism which is levelled primarily against AIR's Regional News bulletins broadcast from the stations, it applies to some extent to news which is centrally originated. A glance at Indian newspapers will show that the criticism applies equally to them, especially to the English language press. The fact is that the Indian news agencies have not developed their machinery for collecting district and local news to any considerable extent.

There has been a similar imbalance in the resources devoted to urban and rural news collection in AIR. There are 351 districts in India but the total number of AIR's district correspondents is only 217. Moreover, these district correspondents are engaged on a part-time basis, are poorly paid and have inadequate resources for news collection outside the town in which they are located. The majority is not professionally trained. In 1977 the Verghese Working Group reported, 'Akashvani certainly needs to expand its network of correspondents to cover every district and major news centre in the country. These correspondents, whether full-time or part-time should be suitably trained and equipped with portable electronic news-gathering devices, including cassette tapes, recorders and portable video-tape recorders which they should be able to operate. They must be mobile and be able to get at the news and get it back to the regional or central news rooms on news bulletins, newsreels, commentaries, and magazine programmes.' All this applies with even greater force to Doordarshan.

Talks and Discussions: The Scope for Dissent

Given its origin in the days of the Empire, and its rapid development during World War II, it was inevitable that AIR should continue to exhibit many of the characteristics of its origin even after Independence. The most deep-rooted of these is censorship. During the war years political commentary meant Allied propaganda and carefully selected individuals broadcast their weekly comments from AIR stations. B.V. Keskar, Minister for Information and Broadcasting from 1952 to 1962, went one better. Political commentaries were broadcast from Delhi alone and relayed throughout the service. Copies of the 'master' script were transmitted to the stations on teleprinter or by post for translation into the regional languages. Delay by a week did not seem to matter! At the time of the Chinese invasion, AIR found itself dreadfully short of experienced political commentators.

Political comment apart, even in talks on general subjects AIR did not give expression to views critical of the government or of any part of the establishment. Government instructions on what could or could not be said over the AIR were issued confidentially to SDs. Station Directors were expected to settle matters 'tactfully' with talkers and writers should they try to transgress the bounds of what was permissible. This situation continued till 1968 when the AIR Code agreed to by the political parties was accepted by the Cabinet and laid on the table in both Houses of Parliament. The Code itself arose out of a furore caused in 1967 when I, as Station Director, Calcutta, refused to broadcast a talk by the Labour Minister of the United Left Front Government on various grounds including the ground that it was in contempt of the judiciary. The proposed talk was subsequently published in two newspapers and led to a suit of subversion and contempt against the Minister in the Calcutta High Court. The Minister had to make a personal appearance in the court which accepted his unqualified apology but fined him five rupees to be paid to a non-political charity.

The AIR Code, which also applies to Doordarshan, was adopted in 1968 and revised in 1970 states:

Broadcasts on All India Radio by individuals will not permit:
1. criticism of friendly countries;
2. attack on religion or communities;
3. anything obscene; or defamatory;
4. incitement to violence or anything against maintenance of law and order;
5. anything amounting to contempt of Court;
6. aspersions against the integrity of the President, Governors and Judiciary;
7. attack on a political party by name;
8. hostile criticism of any State or the Centre; or
9. anything showing disrespect to the Constitution or advocating change in the Constitution by violence; but advocating changes in a constitutional way should not be debarred.

This Code applies to criticism in the nature of personal tirade, either of a friendly Government or of a political party or of the Central Government or any State Government. But it does not debar references to and/or dispassionate discussion of policies pursued by any of them.

On the Code's application, the document in a footnote states:

If a Station Director finds that the above Code has not been respected in any particular or particulars by an intending broadcaster he will draw the latter's attention to the passage objected to. If the intending broadcaster refuses to accept the Station Director's suggestions and modify his script accordingly the Station Director will be justified in rejecting his or her broadcast. Cases of unresolved differences of opinion between a Minister of a State Government and the Station Director about the interpretation of the Code with respect to a talk to be broadcast by the former will be referred to the Minister of Information and Broadcasting, Government of India who will decide finally whether or not any change in the text of the talk was necessary in order to avoid violation of the Code.

Many commentators have not noticed that the restrictions placed on AIR and Doordarshan in the Code are taken from Clause 2 of Article 19 of the Indian Constitution. This Article lays down the fundamental rights, which include freedom of thought and expression. Clause 2 under the Article gives the state the right to impose 'reasonable restrictions' on this right 'in the interests of sovereignty and integrity of India, security of the state, friendly relations with foreign states, public order, decency or morality, or in relation to contempt of court, defamation, or incitement to an offence.'

The strength and the weakness of the Code lies in its vagueness and generality. The Code can be interpreted liberally, as the clarification indicates, and on the other hand it can be read in a literal and narrow manner which would make criticism and discussion impossible. Except for specific restrictions placed by the government as for example, in the cases of the Punjab in 1984-85 and in Assam earlier, the Indian press has been very free. AIR and Doordarshan could be a lot freer than they are, if not equally free but for the timidity of the news and programme staff.

One of the criticisms raised against the Code by Mehra Masani, in her book *Broadcasting and the People*, is that it is entirely negative and cannot be regarded as a substitute for a positive policy for encouraging free and fair debate. This is true. However, the Code has to be viewed in the context of Article 19.1(a) of the Constitution guaranteeing freedom of expression. It is for the people to express themselves freely in accordance with what they actually think, to assert their right to dissent. Masani also fails to mention the proviso that rational criticism of central and state policies is permissible under the Code.

During the declared Emergency between June 1975 and March 1977, press censorship which applied equally to all media was imposed. While it had been one of the recognised functions of AIR to publicise the government's activities, a line was drawn between the government and the party in power and was carefully observed. This distinction was obliterated and there was a determined move to propagate the personality cult. In August 1977 the Janata government presented to Parliament a White Paper on the *Misuse of Mass Media* which describes the adverse impact of the Emergency on broadcasting. In September 1975, the Prime Minister had told Station Directors of AIR that she did not understand what the concept of 'credibility' implied, since there was no doubt that AIR was a department of government and would remain so. The AIR Code was held in abeyance as 'not being feasible in the changed circumstances.' Neither the cabinet nor Parliament was informed of this fact. The Code was revived after the Janata party came to power in 1977.

After Mrs Gandhi returned to power in 1980, the centre has tended to become more and more dictatorial with the result that criticism and opposing points of view find no place in radio and TV. This trend is well reflected in the refusal of the Station Director, Jaipur, to accept the script of a talk by a senior Gandhian scholar, Siddharaj Dhadda, who had been invited to broadcast on 'The Relevance of Gandhi' on his birth anniversary, 2 October 1983. The speaker had drawn attention to differences between Gandhi and Nehru on the concept of planning and had attributed the prevailing widespread poverty and unemployment to the fact that India had rejected the Gandhian way. The speaker was asked to delete the references to Gandhi-Nehru disagreements, poverty and unemployment, all of which he refused to do. The script was subsequently published in the *Indian Express* together with a letter by Mr Dhadda, on 15 October 1983, and commented on four days later.

Another incident about which the press has been reticent, because of the delicate nature of the issues raised, concerns the President. The President, Giani Zail Singh, recorded his annual message for AIR on the eve of Independence Day, 15 August 1986. Apparently some sentences were edited out of the recording and were also removed from the script officially released by the Press Information Bureau. Reportedly, this happened without the prior permission and knowledge of the President. During the Emergency people were scandalised to know that newspaper editors could not publish, without the approval of the Chief Censor, quotations from the writings and speeches of Gandhiji, Nehru and Rabindranath Tagore, including Tagore's poems.

Access: Party Political Broadcasts

While the question of access to AIR by political parties at the time of general elections had been raised in the early fifties, it was not considered seriously till a decade later. The problem was to devise a formula which would be acceptable to all the recognised parties. With the Congress party having an overwhelming majority in Parliament and in the state Assemblies and fielding by far the largest number of candidates, any arrangement based on the number of sitting members and the number of candidates fielded would tilt the scales heavily in its favour. The complaint of the other parties was that the Congress, being the party in power, was in any case able exclusively to propagate and publicise its own programme through AIR under the guise of government information. A formula devised by the Chief Election Commissioner as the basis for discussion was that all recognised parties should have one broadcast each but the Congress party should have a second broadcast at the end of the series which amounted to the right of reply. The opposition parties did not accept this. The Chief Election Commissioner then suggested that each party should make one broadcast and that the Congress party broadcast should come at the end of the series which would enable it as the ruling party to reply to its critics. This proposal was also rejected by the Congress party in 1971. This stalemate continued for over a decade until the Janata party came to power in March 1977 and conceded the principle of equal time to each recognised party. In election broadcasts only the first six clauses of the AIR Code are applicable and, in clause 6, the reference to governors has been deleted. The reason is that a governor may have been responsible for running the administration of a state prior to an election if it were under President's rule and his administration should not be above criticism. The clauses of the Code referred to above were accepted at a meeting of representatives of political parties convened by L.K. Advani, Minister of Information and Broadcasting, in May 1977. This was a momentous step forward in bringing democracy to radio and TV.

Party political broadcasts were arranged, both on radio and TV, during elections to a large number of state legislatures during the summer of 1977. The order in which the parties broadcast was determined by drawing lots at a meeting convened by the Station Director at the state capital. This procedure remains common for radio and TV. Party election broadcasts initiated by the Janata government have ever since been delivered on radio and TV in the same form — straight talks. New formats have not been tried out.

What about opposition parties getting some scope to air their views in the five years between elections? This again was an issue raised in West Bengal, in November 1967. The governor had dismissed the United Left Front Government on 21 November and had sworn in a new ministry under P.C. Ghosh. He had asked the Chief Minister to seek a vote of confidence in the state Assembly which he convened eight days later. The moment the Assembly met the Speaker adjourned it sine die, questioning the validity of the

ULF Ministry's dismissal. In this situation the Chief Minister wanted to record a statement for immediate broadcast. He was allowed to do so, but the Speaker was also given time to put over his version. The principle of 'the right to reply' was thus established for the first time. Unfortunately it did not become a precedent. Ten long years had to pass before the Janata government at the centre accepted the principle that the leader of the opposition should be invited to broadcast both at the centre and in the states, when the Prime Minister and the Chief Ministers spoke at the conclusion of a year in office.

AIR owes the decision of the right of reply in 1967 to the courage and persuasion of Asok Mitra, a well known demographer and scholar, who was at that time Secretary to Government in the I & B Ministry. The Station Director, Calcutta (the author), had recommended to the Director-General and the Minister that, if the Chief Minister were permitted to broadcast, both the Speaker and the leader of the opposition who considered himself wrongfully removed, should be given the right to reply. The suggestion was turned down by the Minister. Mr Mitra could not be contacted at this stage. When he came to know the Minister's decision, he persuaded him to change it and asked AIR to invite the Speaker that very night, to give his reply the next day. The revised decision was given immediate publicity so that the government could not go back on its word even if it had wanted to do so.

Unfortunately, broadcasts by leaders of the opposition were dropped by the Congress party after it returned to power in 1980. Party political broadcasts on a regular basis between elections which were being considered by the Janata Government, never got off the ground because it fell before a decision was taken.

Party political differences merged with centre-state relations in two incidents which occurred in 1980 and in 1983. In the first, the Chief Minister of the southern state of Kerala, who headed a communist-led government, was initially denied an opportunity to speak over the AIR station in Trivandrum, the state capital. The occasion was the second anniversary of his government in office. The Chief Minister went to the press whereupon permission was granted. The second incident occurred in 1983, when the Chief Minister of Andhra Pradesh, N.T. Rama Rao, who was at the head of a non-Congress government, was also denied permission to broadcast on the issue of a strike by non-gazetted government servants. The Chief Minister sent a telex to Mrs Gandhi who immediately gave permission. The late U.L. Baruah, a former DG, writing in the *Statesman* of 25 September 1983 after his retirement, said, 'The hesitation in allowing non-Congress Chief Ministers to broadcast was that of the political masters, and not of the media executives.'

The viewpoint of the non-Congress governments was given at the Information Ministers' Conference held on 6 July 1983. The West Bengal Minister said:

> The two most important tools of opinion formation are AIR and Doordarshan. Both are controlled by the Central Government... The way these two media are being used now leaves much to be desired. The allegation of their partisan use cannot be dismissed lightly. We, in West Bengal, have felt on occasions that there was a serious misconception regarding the priorities of items in the all-India news telecast. There have been occasions when the State Government's news, including policy announcements by the Chief Minister, did not receive the attention due to them on issues where the opposition standpoint got elaborate coverage. I ... request the Central Government to consider how these two media should be made to help the State Governments in accordance with the hopes and aspirations of the people of the states, different linguistic groups, the socially backward and the poor.

In the same conference, the Jammu and Kashmir minister referred to the coverage of the elections in that State and stressed the need for radio and television not appearing to be partisan or arbitrary during elections. The J and K National Conference had, as a protest, refrained from exercising its right to use these media.

Another manifestation of the problem of centre-state relations occurred over the Doordarshan's national programme introduced on 15 August 1982. The service was to be telecast daily by the Delhi centre and relayed by all other centres between 8.30 PM and 10 PM. The Chief Minister of Tamil Nadu called it an attempt to impose Hindi and succeeded in getting the Madras centre to discontinue the relay of Hindi news. The Andhra Pradesh Chief Minister, N.T. Rama Rao, reacted similarly. The Jammu and Kashmir Chief Minister thought that the relay of programmes at the prime viewing time had down-graded the regional language programmes of the Srinagar centre. The Chief Minister of West Bengal felt the same way. Calcutta and Madras telecast for some four and a half hours in all, and regarded the loss of one and a half hours at prime time as an imposition. Moreover, the contents of the national programme are considered poor by viewers, even according to an official survey of TV's audience research department.

Before leaving the subject of centre-state relations, it is important to record an incident which took place in Cuttack, the capital of Orissa, on 27 July 1970. The state government was a coalition dominated by the Swatantra party, a liberal right-wing party (which, after a life of ten years, was to be wiped out in the elections of 1971). An agitation had been developing in which eleven parties including those in power were involved, for the location of a second steel plant in the state. To press their demand, the parties declared a 'bandh' or a total close-down of all activities, government offices, schools, commerce, etc. All this was done with the active support of the government, at whose instance even the telegraph and telephone services (run by the Government of India) were not allowed to function. For the day of the strike Orissa was cut off from the rest of India and the world.

What was to happen to the AIR station at Cuttack and to the auxiliary centre at Sambalpur, some four hundred kms. away? The parties responsible for the bandh asked the Minister of Information and Broadcasting to close down the AIR stations for the day, which he refused to do. The Chief Secretary to the state government, according to a report in the *Statesman* of Calcutta dated 26 July 1970, informed the Government of India, that while it would provide security to the radio stations, 'it would not be advisable for them to carry on the services of which the consequences might be serious.'

Under instructions of the government of India, the Cuttack station commenced its morning transmission at the usual time, 6 AM. As the Oriya newspaper, *Samaj*, reported in its issue of 29 July, a huge crowd had collected at the gates of the station demanding its closure. The paper goes on to state that the Additional District Magistrate on duty, entered the radio station and issued a written order to the Station Director, to close down the transmission as it constituted a 'grave threat to law and order' and might result in 'bloodshed and endanger property.' The paper noted that the station was closed down at 7.46 AM. At Sambalpur, mobs attacked the transmitter, smashed windows and threatened to damage the equipment. The police stood by and watched. The programme was stopped at 9.30 AM. Cuttack and Sambalpur remained off the air for the rest of the day.

The Ministry of Information and Broadcasting then took an extraordinary step; it suspended the Station Director, R.N. Das, and issued him with a charge-sheet. His offence was a failure to keep the transmission going in accordance with the orders given to him. According to government disciplinary procedure, a preliminary inquiry investigates the matter and, on the basis of its findings, a decision is taken on the framing of charges. However, before the report was submitted, the Ministry took action. The case was heard. Mr Das pleaded not guilty and argued that if he had not complied with the magistrate's order he would have been guilty of contempt of court and would have been liable to imprisonment. After two years of travail, he was exonerated.

The Ministry of Information and Broadcasting sought advice from the Ministry of Law in case such a situation were to recur. Its advice was that a Station Director would have to comply with a magistrate's order but that he could apply immediately to the High Court for the vacation of the order! How such action could be taken in towns where a High Court does not exist or when the court is in vacation are questions which AIR raised. A question raised by the Ministry was whether it is legal for a magistrate to pass an order which directs a government servant to desist from discharging his official duties? Officials of the Ministry, far removed from the scene of action, shouldering no real responsibility, could indeed afford to quibble about such matters, on which in any case AIR received no answers. Happily a direct confrontation, where the state government stops AIR or Doordarshan from functioning, has not arisen again.

Social Issues

Since Independence, a platform has been provided by AIR/Doordarshan for social causes as a result of two factors. Under government aegis, a large number of days and weeks are observed in the course of the year, such as, Wild Life Week, Anti-Leprosy Day, Vana Mahotsav (tree plantation) Week. At one stage the number of 'days' to be observed far exceeded the number of days in the calendar! More recently, under UNESCO's auspices, AIR and Doordarshan have been devoting a whole year to such matters as

Family Planning and Women and Children. On such occasions, government is anxious to give publicity to these themes and positive directives are issued by government to the media. Representatives of the organisations involved are invited to broadcast programmes. Second, individuals who have been personally concerned with social welfare, animal welfare, the environment ·and so on have approached government for media publicity. These social groups while concerned to take advantage of official channels are not interested in the principle of access as such.

In the early seventies, AIR decided to invite outsiders, through public advertisement, to contribute complete programmes which could be bought as finished products for broadcast. Individuals were requested to write to the stations indicating the subjects or themes which they proposed to take up and to discuss further details with Station Directors. The few letters received were from persons who had no definite ideas on the programmes they wanted to produce. Considering that the absence of production facilities might have been a reason for the poor response, AIR advertised a second time and indicated that it would provide technical facilities.

Again the response was negative. The meagre payment offered was probably responsible Since 1980, with the growing tendency to stamp out dissent from AIR, there has been less and less place for access for private groups.

With very limited hours of transmission till 1982, there was little scope for access programmes on Doordarshan by outside producers. However, for a period of some six months commencing October 1985, Doordarshan had a brief flirtation with dissent through access. It was heralded by a fortnightly programme *Newsline* presented by M.J. Akbar, well-known for his recent book *India: The Siege Within* (Penguin). The programme started probing scandals in Congress and non-Congress states alike. Some Chief Ministers demanded time on Doordarshan to present their side of the picture which was, of course, given. Also at about the same time Doordarshan on its own started a programme entitled *Sach Ki Parchain* (Shadows of Truth) which gave evidence of social concern. The first programme was on the police which provoked much favorable response for its frankness. Other programmes highlighted the working of the railways, and the Delhi Development Authority which is responsible for providing housing to citizens.

This spree did not last. There were reports that political pressure was being brought to bear through the sponsors of *Newsline* to tone down the criticism of government. Then the end came. *Newsline* was taken off and *Sach Ki Parchain* lost its bite. Thereafter two events have occurred which have put paid to any form of dissent. On 7 February 1986, after repeated announcements that Doordarshan would telecast that very night a documentary *Rajiv's India* by the well-known American producer Jack Anderson, the programme did not appear on the screen. No explanation was given to the public as to the grounds for this sudden change in the government's decision. The strange fact is that the documentary had been previewed by the press at a largely attended gathering in Delhi where the Minister of Information and Broadcasting was present. It is believed by many that the programme was cancelled because of critical remarks made by R.N. Goenka, the proprietor of the Express group of papers, about Mrs Indira Gandhi for imposing the Emergency in 1975. What he said was that although he had been a friend of Mrs Gandhi for many years, he thought she went astray in imposing the Emergency. He added that he was confident that under the leadership of Rajiv Gandhi, the future of India was safe.

Hardly had this incident passed off when another occurred on 2 March. This time it was over a film, *New Delhi Times*, the first production of Ramesh Sharma. Here again the telecast was widely advertised and withdrawn at the last minute. No explanation was given by Doordarshan. Subsequently this film won a National Award in the annual Indian Film Festival (also held under the auspices of the I & B Ministry) and later it was adjudged the best first film by a young director at Karlovy Vary. The film ran at public cinema houses in Delhi for several weeks and was seen by thousands of people. It is concerned with the manner in which big business is behind communal riots in this country and how the press can be manipulated when it comes into conflict with vested interests in league with politicians. There are scenes of mob violence, arson and looting but they are intended to arouse sympathy for human beings of all communities who are the victims of such holocausts. It was widely believed that in both these cases cancellation was due to the interference of powerful political personalities outside the government, who intervened over the head of the Minister of I & B.

However, one serial supposedly devoted to social criticism, was able to run its course. This was a weekly programme entitled *Rajni*, produced in Bombay and telecast over the network at noon on Sundays. Rajni, a very well-turned out young woman, was the central character who set out to expose social abuses. One week it was the extortion practised by taxi drivers, another the bribery and corruption in the telephone department, or the exploitation of domestic child labour. I would describe these programmes as the Indian film variety of social escapism. The only person caught for corruption in the telephone service was on the lowest rung of the ladder. The wealthy couple who gave the bribes went scot-free; they were not even held up for public scorn. Everything ended happily; a character representing the government told us that such things would not happen again! All this is not surprising when one realises that *Rajni* was a programme sponsored by a big business house.

The most difficult problem for developing countries is to give access to the vast numbers of society who through ignorance and illiteracy are not aware of their own rights and who are therefore exploited by vested interests despite the laws on the statute books. Because of the lack of financial and other resources these groups are unable to organise themselves. For them, access must be arranged by others. To some extent this can be done by social workers or sociologists who spend long periods with different peoples, get to know their real problems and win their confidence. AIR has been in touch with a few such persons who have been responsible for moving programmes. In the late seventies, a series was started in the National Programme entitled *My Village*. But it was a flash in the pan.

Apart from making use of outside agencies to provide access, AIR has itself attempted over the past decade or so to shoulder this responsibility. The best known of these programmes, broadcast daily from Srinagar Station, is entitled *Zoona Dab* which means 'Moon on the Courtyard'. It started in the late sixties and has continued since. The programme has dealt mainly with problems of the inhabitants of Srinagar city brought to the notice of the station by poor, downtrodden and often illiterate people. Most stations started regularly broadcasting programmes of this kind, in the period 1973-75 prior to the Emergency. One series dealt with the difficulties of illiterate people in securing medical attention in Delhi and its neighbouring rural areas. A particularly pertinent programme showed that the most consistent donors to the blood bank in Delhi were the 'thelawallas' or handcart pullers. Donors are paid a pittance for each donation and in many cases the handcart pullers, underfed and anaemic, with little other means of livelihood, were returning to give repeated donations at intervals far shorter than stipulated by the health authorities. These programmes raised a storm of protest from the Ministry of Health, but the Information and Broadcasting Ministry stood firm, arguing that the programmes were in the best interests of society and government itself.

The outstanding popularity gained by the Srinagar station's programme has been due to the backing it has consistently received from the highest authority in the state. If a complaint was voiced in the programme it was attended to without delay. This was because the Chief Minister in the early 1970s listened regularly and questioned officials on action taken on the complaints voiced in the programme. In contrast with this cooperative attitude, many state governments do not wish to give information to the public and as a result officials refuse to participate in programmes. In such a situation the need to expose those who stand in the way of providing information to the public was tried out in just one instance. There was no reaction either way.

In short, steps to facilitate access have been halting and there were shortcomings which have to be recorded. Access was available only in the cities where AIR stations are located, and no special resources were earmarked for access programmes. Stations had to find money for them after meeting their mandatory commitments; access programmes themselves were never mandatory. Most importantly the planning of access programmes, their duration, frequency and format were decided entirely by AIR stations. There was no public participation in the planning process and no system for determining the total number of access programmes and their allocation between different groups. All this applied equally to Doordarshan. The Director-General said at a public meeting in New Delhi in November 1985 that, while he could not set aside time for access programmes, he would consider what was offered and pay as generously as possible within the system. The meeting had been arranged under the auspices of the Indo-US Committee for cooperation in the fields of radio, TV, and film, to view and discuss the possibilities of video.

The inadequate attention that has been paid to access in Indian broadcasting is undoubtedly bound up with the fact that it has functioned under government control.

Government Information and Development Support

In the First Five Year Plan document in 1951 government defined the role of communications in development thus:

> A widespread understanding of the Plan is an essential stage in its fulfilment. An understanding of the priorities of the Plan will enable each person to relate his or her role to the larger purposes of the nation as a whole. All available methods of communication have to be developed and the people approached through the written and spoken word no less than through radio, film, song and drama.

AIR took up this job through various programmes, especially in the rural, tribal and educational programmes. News was, of course, very important. During and immediately after national calamities, such as floods and cyclones, AIR has often been the only means of communication between the government and the people. AIR transmitters have been on the air round the clock.

Perhaps the most important of resources for development are the Rural Programmes. Through the years various strategies have been tried out. The experiment in Radio Rural Forums held in Poona from February to April 1956 has already been mentioned. It was based on the Canadian model and designed to establish two-way communication between village audiences and the programmers of the radio station. A forum consisting of about twenty persons was set up, one each in 150 selected villages. Each forum had a chairman, who presided and kept order, and a secretary who was provided with a small sum of money for stationery and postage. Once every week the Poona station broadcast a special half-hour programme for the forums. The first twenty minutes were devoted to a specific topic such as rice cultivation and the remaining time to answering questions. Members of the forum were expected to listen to the programme together at the community listening centre. After the programme was over they discussed what had been said in the topic for the day. Doubts and queries were raised and comments made. If the members could not solve them on their own, the secretary jotted down the points and wrote to the programme organiser at the station for advice. On his part, the programme organiser sought out the experts in the Agriculture Department of the state government and obtained their guidance. Queries raised in one programme

were answered in the last ten minutes of the next one. Twenty programmes were broadcast in the course of the experiment.

The experiment was devised to ascertain:

(a) Whether Radio Rural Forums could be used for the transmission of knowledge.

(b) Whether group discussion was an efficient method for this
purpose.

(c) Whether the Radio Rural Forums could be a new institution in
the life of the village.

(d) The reaction of the forum members to Radio Farm Forums as
a whole.

A group of social scientists under Dr Paul Neurath of UNESCO
conducted the evaluation. The report was fulsome in its praise:

> ... a success beyond expectations. Increase in knowledge in the
> forum villages ... was spectacular, whereas in the non-forum
> villages it was negligible. Forums developed rapidly into deci-
> sion-making bodies capable of speeding up common pursuits in
> the village faster than the elected panchayat. Frequently they
> took on functions half way between those of a panchayat and a
> town meeting. The forums thus became an important instrument
> of village democracy ... .

As a result of the experiment it was decided, in 1959, to establish
forums at all stations. Encouraged by government, more and more
forums were set up, and the frequency of the programme was
increased from one to two a week. In 1964 it was claimed that there
were 7,500 forums in the country. Between 1959 and 1964 there
were approximately thirty radio stations in the country, which
means that there were 350 forums per station! After 1964, almost
nothing is heard about the forums. There is occasional talk of
'charcha mandalis,' small groups who are said to gather round a
transistor set and to listen to and discuss programmes. But in effect
forums have faded out. It has been contended that this is the result
of the transistor revolution. With transistors available cheaply,
group listening has given place to individual listening; people prefer
to listen in their homes rather than trudge to the community listening
set. However, in addition to this factor, I believe that the great
increase in the number of forums was responsible for their decay. If
the forums increased beyond a certain number, it became impossible
for the station to maintain close personal contact, answer questions

in reasonable time and so on. When this happened the forums inevitably lost interest. It would have been wiser to keep down the number of forums and to run a forum for a limited period, say a year. Thereafter, forums could be set up in different groups of villages. The forum should have been treated as a ginger group. If it took root in the village it would have carried on without official support.

Since then various other ideas have been tried out. An effort is made to include field-based material in the programmes. Demonstrations conducted by agricultural workers are reported. Farmers are interviewed on the spot to ascertain what they have learned, and their questions and doubts are answered; the whole exercise is recorded and the recording broadcast in the programme for the benefit of the farming community as a whole. To facilitate this work Farm and Home Units have been set up at stations under a Farm Radio Officer. The unit includes a recordist, a scriptwriter and is provided with its own jeep.

In the early seventies some stations in the south started a programme called 'Farm School of the Air'. The programme consisted of a complete course on some subject of relevance to farmers. The programme was modelled on the lines of the forum broadcasts, with a question and answer session to conclude it. What was new was that listeners had to register themselves with the station and only queries sent in by registered persons are replied to in the programmes. In 1978 the Bangalore station announced that they would hold a written examination which would be open to registered listeners. Over 20,000 persons applied to sit in the test. The Agriculture University, Bangalore, helped in conducting the examination. A number of private agencies offered to give valuable prizes such as a pair of bullocks for the first prize; spraying equipment, incubators, and a hundred chicks as consolation prizes. The first prize-giving ceremony in Bangalore was a regular fair. Farmers from distant villages came to attend it. There was much enthusiasm. Since then the 'Farm School of the Air' is being run at a number of stations and prize distributions are being organised.

A sobering fact becoming increasingly evident to farm broadcasters, is that radio provides maximum benefit to farmers who are relatively affluent and well-educated. The claim of radio to break through the barrier of illiteracy has proved marginal. Dr K.N. Singh of the Indian Council of Agricultural Research (India) in a valuable paper, 'Communicating with Rural People' (1975), tells us that affluent and educated farmers consider information received through the radio next only in value to that which they get from the agricultural experts. On the other hand, the poor and illiterate farmer depends for advice on agricultural demonstrations, observation of the practice of 'progressive' farmers, specialists, extension agents, television and radio, in that order. He needs information and advice frequently and cheaply, which radio could provide. But illiteracy and lack of an adequate educational background stand in the way of his using such information to his best advantage.

There has been some criticism in the press and in public forums to the effect that AIR's programmes are urban-oriented; 6.3 per cent of transmission time devoted to nearly 80 per cent of the population is manifestly unjust. There is some validity in this complaint. On the other hand it has to be counterbalanced by the fact that due to poverty and other factors, the bulk of AIR's actual audience lives in the cities. Moreover, the 'do-gooders', of whom there is no dearth within government and outside, fail to recognise that the lack of entertainment is one of the important problems of rural life. There is nothing to show that so-called urban entertainment such as film songs, drama and classical music are not enjoyed by rural folk. The overemphasis on an 'uplifting message' in every programme, very evident during the Emergency and ever lurking in the wings, is self-defeating and constitutes a danger which has to be guarded against.

Tribal Programmes

Tribal programmes are broadcast in various dialects in the tribal regions. In content they may be compared with Rural Programmes except that they also include a short news bulletin and entertainment items of folk music and tribal culture. Spoken-word tribal programmes go out in fifty dialects.

The government's policy is to broadcast to the tribal people in their own dialects in the belief that this is the only way to speak to them directly. However, it creates problems. Let us take the case of Nagaland where the problem is most acute. There is one radio station in this state located at Kohima the capital. There are sixteen major dialects, and the station is already broadcasting programmes in thirteen of them. In addition there are programmes in Nagamese, a sort of bazaar language which is the lingua franca of Nagaland.

and in English for the intelligentsia, such as relays of English news bulletins from Delhi, National Programme talks, commentaries and also some locally originated programmes. The programmes in dialects range from fifteen to twenty-five minutes per day. The four largest tribes constitute respectively 17.3 per cent, 16.9 per cent and 15 per cent of the population. The others are much smaller, and in the case of the smallest only 1.4 per cent of the population. So when a dialect programme is on the air a vast proportion of Naga listeners are unable to comprehend it.

It has been argued that the solution to this problem is technical. Instead of sharing time on one transmitter, we should set up thirteen transmitters, though this would be an expensive proposition. My reply is that there would be a wastage of transmitters. We have to remember that frequencies are limited and it would be folly to use up so many frequencies on a population of approximately five hundred thousand.

Apart from the question of wastage, my basic contention is that it is not effective. My argument is twofold. Firstly, that because of the limitations of language, one cannot express in the dialects the sort of things that commonly form the subject matter of such spoken word items as news, commentary and talks on utility subjects. Secondly, I want to contend that the sort of things that are talked about in such programmes cannot be assimilated. Let me try and elucidate these arguments.

It seems to me evident that the language of communication must have a significant relationship with the medium of instruction. The linguistic policy of AIR in Nagaland, however, bears no relationship to the policy followed in regard to the medium of instruction. English is the official language of the state, and even at the primary level English is supposed to be the medium of instruction; although from what I have been able to gather, an attempt is being made to provide primary instruction for the first two years in a few of the major dialects such as Ao and Angami. But there are difficulties because there are no books in these dialects. If the Naga dialects are to develop, an effort must be made to produce books in them. New words have to be coined, syntax has to be developed and refined to make language flexible enough to present varied concepts and the many relationships they bear to each other. It is strange indeed that we should hold, on the one hand, that a dialect is not developed enough for the purpose of primary education, and on the other, that we can use it to present, what in the nature of the case must be, fairly sophisticated ideas which crop up in a news bulletin. This lack of coordination between a language policy in education and mass communication exists also in Meghalaya and Manipur.

The question arises: what is the degree of development of the Naga dialects? A study of about a dozen dictionaries compiled by the Nagaland Bhasha Parishad, Kohima, reveals that the total number of words in any of the dialects does not exceed five thousand and in some, three thousand. The vast majority of the words are common nouns. In most cases the Naga word is actually a Hindi or Assamese word. Normally, a large section of a vocabulary is taken up with abstract nouns. But even in the case of a commonly used abstract noun such as love, the Naga dialects seem to lack words which denote the concept. The Naga equivalents take the form of the verb 'to be'. Love means 'to make love'. It has been well said that one could live in a Naga village for a month without hearing an abstract term.

J.P. Mills in a long and comprehensive chapter on 'Language' in his book the *Ao Nagas* (1926) remarks: 'The Ao lives a hard practical life and the language which he has evolved to meet his needs is a practical one which does not deal with abstractions and philosophical generalisations. An Ao would never say "Lenti has a universal reputation for hospitality" but "All men say Lenti feeds guests well".' What was true when Mills wrote seems to be equally true today sixty years later.

It is on these grounds that I contend that the dialects are not a satisfactory vehicle for conveying information and ideas through radio.

My second contention hinges on the ability of the persons in the target audience to assimilate the information provided to them. Information, if it is to be assimilated, has to fit into a framework of knowledge which the person already possesses. If the basic frame is missing, the information supplied will not be understood and will be lost.

Let me summarise the argument. The object of using the dialects is to reach the common man in the Naga village. We use the dialect because we believe that he knows no other language. He is illiterate and has had no formal education. He has not travelled much, hardly ever beyond his own district, because had he done so he would perforce have picked up some other language such as Nagamese.

My contention is that a person with such a background, confined to his own culture and custom, does not have the framework of knowledge in which information and ideas thrown at him in radio news bulletins and talks can be assimilated.

To test the validity of this hypothesis a limited study was undertaken at my instance by AIR's Audience Research Department in Nagaland in 1974. A field-cum-laboratory technique was employed in four areas of the state, speaking the Angami, Ao, Chang and Sema dialects.

A number of items selected from news bulletins and talks in the four dialects were recorded and played back, each to two different groups comprising persons speaking each dialect. One group consisted of villagers who were either illiterate, or educated up to the secondary level; while the other group consisted of town folk such as a civil surgeon, a district publicity officer, an office-bearer of a town committee, a college lecturer and students at the graduate and post-graduate level etc. The items played back included short talks, on subjects such as (*i*) a national level essay competition in connection with International Women's Year; (*ii*) a talk on family planning; (*iii*) women in the Indian national movement; (*iv*) people's participation in a rural development project in Vaishal, and (*v*) hints on nutrition. News items selected for playback included (*i*) the construction of a cooperative society building in the village Khaliga at a cost of Rs 18.000; (*ii*) the lifting of curfew in Mizoram; (*iii*) report of a speech delivered by Vice-President Jatti; (*iv*) report of an agreement signed between Tanzania and India; and (*v*) report about a proposed visit of a Naga choir to foreign countries.

After the playback of items to each group, the observations of individuals on their understanding of each item and the language used were noted and there was also a discussion on their reaction to the news items and short talks.

The findings of a study of this kind, severely limited as it was, cannot be taken as final. It is always possible to argue that a subject such as spacing of children could have been presented differently in a simpler and more explanatory fashion. Nevertheless, some of the conclusions of the study are worth pondering over.

One of the prime findings was that there was very considerable use of English words. This was criticised by both the village level and townsfolk groups. This use of English words militated against comprehension.

The general comprehension of news, particularly at the village level, was severely limited. News items carrying the names of persons and places and referring to subjects with which the villager was unacquainted, made little sense to him. No one in either of the groups, including educated persons, recognised the name of B.D. Jatti, though some knew that there is such an office as Vice-President of India. A few in the townsfolk group were aware that Pondicherry is in India. The survey observed that, while the villager's restricted knowledge creates in him a desire to expand it, it does not give him the capacity to assimilate information which is not related to his own surroundings.

Concepts such as stoppage of child birth, spacing of children, use of vitamins in diet, were not easily assimilable even by the town group, especially if presented in a theoretical fashion.

It may be objected that my argument is wholly negative. If we are not to broadcast in the dialects, then what are we to do and how do we expect to reach the common man? What is it that I recommend as a substitute and on what basis?

My suggestion is that in Nagaland we should broadcast in two languages only — Nagamese and English. By this I mean that the spoken word programmes originating at Kohima should be confined to these languages. Of course folk and light songs in the dialects, Hindi film music etc. should continue.

Programmes from the station should be broadcast at two levels. The mass audience programmes should be in Nagamese. These should include news pertaining to Nagaland and the neighbouring hill states and Assam. Events occurring in the border areas of Burma, Tibet and China could also be included. Commentaries on local developments, political and economic, could be covered. Other spoken word programmes should be on agriculture, animal husbandry, poultry, crafts and so on. Of course health and connected problems should also be dealt with.

Another group of programmes to be broadcast in English, should be addressed to the town folk and to those at various educational levels. News for such persons could deal with national and international issues and in fact, commentaries, talks, discussion and other such programmes should be addressed to a middle level of sophistication. The relays from Delhi would meet the needs of the élite.

It would be argued that broadcasting organised in this way might be an investment in the future. In a decade or so, with more youngsters in schools, it might pay dividends. But what of today? How will your villager confined to his Konyak or Chang village profit? It is a commonplace of communication research, that the educated and literate members of the community read the daily newspaper and comprehend the radio broadcasts. Dissemination of news and information is passed onto them through face to face communication to the community as a whole. A good deal of interpretation and explanation in response to doubts and queries, is provided in the process. This happens today when we broadcast in the dialects and would happen in future if we restrict broadcasting to Nagamese and English.

Other studies conducted by AIR's Audience Research Department have shown that the BBC's World Service is the most popular of foreign broadcasting services among the Nagas. They also listen to programmes from Bangladesh and Pakistan. Western music is what attracts the common listener. The intelligentsia among the tribals pick up what is of interest to them in the news and comment, and the gist of it finds its way to others. In tribal areas AIR must depend on the two-step flow of information, which is crucial with audiences where literacy is not widespread.

Local Radio

An important step taken by AIR in development support programming was the setting up of a 'local' radio station at Nagercoil in Tamil Nadu in November 1984. This station, with a one KWT transmitter, has been given almost complete autonomy, atleast on paper, from the policy framework of AIR stations. Its function is to provide area-specific programmes and to demolish the division between the broadcaster and the audience. The station's emphasis is on field-based programmes and it is supposed to cover every village in the district in turn. Farming, rural development, health, family welfare, and education are the topics of transmission. Much attention is to be paid to access: opportunities are to be given to distinct groups to present their own programmes affording scope for the articulation of local talent. At the time of writing, this local station had completed just one year of its life and no information is available on how it had functioned and what problems it had encountered. It will be interesting to know how it gets on. Four 'local' stations are to be set up in the Seventh Plan.

SITE and After

Undoubtedly the most important step taken by the government to harness broadcasting for development was SITE.

Vikram Sarabhai, one of India's distinguished physicists and educationists, who was head of the Atomic Energy department until his sudden death in 1971, was the chief sponsor and champion of SITE. It was Dr Sarabhai who signed the agreement with NASA on India's behalf. He defined its objectiveness in the following words:

If India wants to reduce the overwhelming attraction of immigration to cities, enrich cultural life, integrate the country by exposing one part to the cultures of the other parts, involve people in the programme of rural, economic and social development, then the best thing is to have TV via a satellite.

The main criterion for the deployment of the available direct reception TV receivers was backwardness. The Planning Commission in its Fifth Plan (1975-79) document, in the chapter dealing with the development of backward areas laid down some fifteen indicators to identify economically backward areas. This list of indicators included such factors as density of population, percentage of irrigated area/cultivable area for agricultural workers, number of workers employed in factories, availability of electricity, mileage of surfaced roads, literacy, technical training facilities and hospitals.

However, when it came to the precise location of the sets, the considerations which applied were:

(a) availability of electricity;
(b) distance from the maintenance centre;
(c) population;
(d) agricultural, educational, health and family planning infrastructures; and
(e) supporting facilities, such as all-weather approachability by road.

No doubt political pressures played their part, with the result that one could find half a dozen TV sets on or just off the main road within a radius of 25 kilometres of a capital city.

While NASA provided the satellite, on the Indian side two agencies were responsible for SITE. The Indian Space Research Organisation (ISRO) were responsible for setting up and maintaining the up-link both at Ahmedabad and Delhi. The installation and maintenance of the special receivers were also their responsibilities. In order to receive the programme direct from the satellite an ordinary domestic receiver had to be altered in two special directions. A special type of antenna, known as a chicken-mesh antenna, rather like an umbrella, had to be provided for each receiver.

Doordarshan, which was then part of AIR, was mainly responsible for the programmes. The programmes, which were largely field-based, carried a common picture for two adjoining cluster groups, but each group had its own audio channel. Thus, for example, it was thought that a picture taken in Karnataka would be sufficiently close to one taken in Andhra and could therefore be used for clusters in both regions without loss of authenticity. Two sound tracks were provided to meet the needs in the two different linguistic regions. This made for economy but it meant that talking was one-way: dialogue or the direct exchange of information or the clarification that comes from questions and answers could not be achieved in such programmes. Questions and answers had to be built into the commentary.

Programmes were telecast in two transmissions, morning and evening. The evening programme provided half an hour for each cluster group in its own language. Apart from agricultural information, health and family planning were the chief educational subjects. Entertainment, consisting of drama, dance and music, particularly folk and rural art-forms drawn from the region and outside, completed the tally. National integration, it was hoped, would be helped by people getting to know more about each other. In the morning each linguistic group received a programme of a little over twenty minutes, designed for children between the ages of five and twelve years. It was intended as an enrichment programme and was not tied to the school syllabus. One of its chief objectives was to provide some colour and excitement in village schools which are accused of being intolerably dull and where the drop-out rate is alarmingly high. Some of the science programmes were provided by ISRO.

SITE was launched with much fanfare by the then Prime Minister, Indira Gandhi, on 1 August 1975 and it continued till 31 July 1976. The quality of the picture and the sound was excellent throughout the country. The programmes went on the air without fail in accordance with the schedule and there was not a single day's breakdown in the service. In August, when the programme started, there had been widespread rain and floods in north Bihar and many sets in the area were affected. Also in the early days there were complaints of fuses blowing due to fluctuations in the voltage. But things soon settled down. ISRO claimed that 90 per cent of the sets worked on any one day. This claim could be exaggerated; but if it is established that 60 to 70 per cent of the sets worked on an average day it would be no mean achievement.

Responsibility for evaluation was entrusted to ISRO, who employed teams of social anthropologists to remain in the cluster areas before the experiment started and beyond, to produce a massive evaluation report, which runs into two volumes. For all its poor writing it is nevertheless the best public document we have of the impact of broadcasting on the people. The Planning Commission also conducted studies, but these were not published. Fortunately the findings have been summarised by Krishen Sondhi in his valuable book *Communication, Growth and Public Policy* (1983).

After the first few months when the novelty of TV wore off the average attendance at sets settled down to about 100 persons. This figure represents the total number of persons who were present for some time during the transmission and it is not suggested that all or even half of them sat right through each programme. Half the total audience consisted of children and youngsters; there were fewer women than men. A substantial proportion of viewers of both sexes belonged to the lower economic and social categories. Among frequent viewers, about half the males were in the age-group of 15 to 24, and 35 per cent of the women were in the age-group of 25 to 39 years.

Sondhi gives us useful statistical data. Only 61 per cent of the villagers viewed a programme even once; 19 per cent were frequent viewers, that is, saw programmes at least three times a week; 21 per cent claimed good comprehension of the programmes. However, only 1 per cent of the adopters of fertilisers said that TV was the first source of their information and 7 per cent stated that it was the main source of their motivation.

The Planning Commission set up a panel to judge the quality of hard core programmes in terms of objectives and clarity in presentation of messages and came to the conclusion that the agriculture programmes were better than the others. The preferences of viewers of various programmes is given in Table 4.1.

The ISRO Report in its foreword states that farmers only adopted those practices which did not demand additional financial outlays.

Table 4.1

Satellite Instructional Television Experiment
Preferred Programmes (Nov. – Dec. 1975)

Programmes	Percentage
Agriculture	74.5
Cultural	39.00
Health and Nutrition	26.6
Family Planning	22.00
All Programmes	16.8
News	9.8

Note: The percentages add up to more than 100 because of multiple responses.

They were also secretive about their intentions until they achieved success. A few new practices were adopted as a result of TV viewing but the extent to which this occurred was not statistically significant. The table given by Sondhi on the adoption of High-Yielding Varieties graphically illustrates the position. (See Table 4.2).

Table 4.2

Number of New HYV Seeds Used by Cultivating
Households for the First Time Between 1 August 1975 and 31 July 1976

	All	States
	Exp.	*Control*
Has not used any new method	85.4%	86.7%
Used one variety of HYV Seeds	6.5%	5.8%
Used two varieties of HYV Seeds	5.2%	4.6%
Used three varieties of HYV Seeds	2.4%	2.3%
Used four varieties of HYV Seeds	0.4%	0.5%
	100.0%	100.0%

One reason given by ISRO for the limited gain was that the villagers had already learnt about these varieties and improved techniques through radio. On the other hand, as in animal husbandry where the techniques themselves were new and not much had been done to propagate them on radio, the villagers gained more from SITE.

One of the inherent weaknesses of SITE was that each language programme was common to a vast area. Thus a programme on cotton cultivation would have little relevance to viewers near Jaipur, though it would be of considerable interest to audiences in Kota, both in Rajasthan. In fact, cropping patterns differ widely from district to district in this country. What the people need is that programmes should meet their local requirements. SITE was hardly an instrument to answer such needs. Lack of interest in some farm programmes was undoubtedly due to this factor. Moreover, farming is a highly localised activity. Various steps such as preparing the soil, sowing, watering, etc., must follow in sequence at the right time. A sudden change in weather conditions might necessitate a change in the normal time table. Unless the telecasting system is local and can respond to such changes quickly it is as good as useless.

In regard to health we learn that there were modest gains during the SITE year. The ISRO evaluators comment that medicines, drugs and other facilities were in short supply and this inevitably limited people's ability to use them. For example, the practice of seeking medical assistance for the delivery of babies was 'minimal'. The survey explains that there were two factors for this poor impact; medical staff were not posted in the villages or sufficiently near at hand, and where they were, the villagers could not afford to pay for their services. On nutrition, the social scientists were unable to collect data.

Regarding family planning, the adoption of vasectomy in the SITE villages was between 2 and 4 per cent higher than in the control villages. But the report considers that these figures might be somewhat inflated. It will be recalled that SITE took place during the Emergency and that the Government had fixed targets for vasectomy which doctors had to achieve. Moreover, a monetary incentive was provided to those who underwent the operation. Considered as a whole increased adoption of family planning techniques as a result of viewing TV is said to have been 'statistically not significant'.

SITE appeared to have an immediate effect on the village schools. The SITE lessons were crowded with students, young and old. The elders started taking an interest in the school buildings and money was found for much-needed repairs. Learning in Indian schools, which is largely rote learning from textbooks, became alive and vivid. However, the SITE Evaluation Report states that the drop-out rate did not fall as a result of TV viewing. This would tend to show that drop-out from the educational system is due to external factors such as economic conditions.

Apart from the hard-core subjects dealt with in SITE, the transmission also included a news bulletin, information on the twenty-point programme and other subjects and cultural items about different parts of the country. To what extent did these programmes increase empathy, create satisfaction or dissatisfaction with rural and social life? Sondhi summarises the conclusions of the Planning Commis-. sion's Study under various heads such as Levels of Empathy, Satisfaction with Aspects of Life, Aspirations for Sons (unfortunately nothing about Daughters!), Perception of the Development Needs of the village and of Government Impact, and Support for the Government and Political Orientation. The general conclusion arrived at by him is that SITE had little effect, positive or negative. It neither created aspirations and expectations, nor did it lead to frustrations. TV was neither the first source of information, nor the main motivating factor for the adoption of new practices in the hard-core areas. Ninety per cent of the information gained and the new practices adopted were the result of interpersonal communication — that is from contact with Village-Level Workers, friends and neighbours. TV did not help to cross the illiteracy barrier. As already reported 39 per cent of the people in the experimental villages never viewed a single programme of SITE. Of these 46 per cent were illiterates; only 13 per cent of illiterates were frequent viewers. Those with primary education accounted for 30 per cent of the total audience, 47 per cent comprised persons with education above the primary level.

Some of the reasons for the poor results achieved by SITE have already been indicated. It is necessary, however, to pinpoint them.

SITE was not properly organised as a systems approach to the problems of rural development. Instructions had been issued for the formation of tele-clubs in the experimental villages, so that programmes could be discussed and two-way communication established between the audience and the programme organisers. This was not done. The Block Development Officer (BDO) and the Village Level Worker (VLW) and others did not see the programmes and therefore could not discuss them with the farmers and other folk. Contact between the BDO/VLW and the audiences which should have been close in order to reinforce through interpersonal communication what was being advocated on the screen was in any case very poor. The Planning Commission Studies show that over a period of six months contact between the change agents and villagers was as follows:

Table 4.3

Contacts with Change-Agents During Six Months
(Nov. – Dec. 1975)

Frequency	VLW%	BDO%
Never	81.11	94.70
Once	2.64	1.39
Twice	4.17	2.36
3 times	3.19	0.14
4 times	1.39	0.56
5 times	0.97	0.00
6 times	1.67	0.42
7 times	4.86	0.43

To sum up: the results achieved as a result of SITE were poor because first, communication can only produce results if a certain minimum level of affluence exists among the audience who can therefore come within the ambit of communications. Unless this basic level is assumed persons cannot make the necessary investment to act on the information they receive from mass media. Second, the efficacy of mass media to achieve results is closely linked with literacy and education. The widely prevalent and persistent belief among TV and radio practitioners that the picture and the spoken word, will cross the illiteracy barrier is a myth which must be demolished. It has already done considerable damage to the cause of development. Third, development can only occur if there is a closely integrated approach with all the required inputs provided and coordinated. It is a mistake to believe, as Lerner has pointed out, that any one or two preferred inputs will bring about the desired result. Fourth, solutions cannot be imposed from above. They must be generated from within the audience, which means in effect that programmes have to be local, for that is the only way to ensure audience participation. Regretably, the Ministry of Infomation and Broadcasting appears to have learnt little from SITE The SITE continuity centres have not modified their presentations to take note of these findings, and as for the Delhi Doordarshan

Kendra's Krishi Darshan (rural programme) it is being relayed to large parts of the country where the picture is irrelevant and the language is not understood!

National Integration and the Development of National Consciousness

The idea of nation-building through broadcasting has been evolving through the decades. The creation of national consciousness or national integration is a major problem in a country as diverse as India with its many languages, cultural traditions and ethnic groups. One method of attempting to achieve this through radio is by presenting the literature, drama and music of each region to all other regions. Thus, AIR has been broadcasting national programmes covering music, drama, features and literary symposia. National Programmes, as mentioned in chapter 3 earlier, are the responsibility of the Chief Producers and Directors of Programmes at the Directorate-General, planned by them in consultation with the stations. Production may be undertaken by a Chief Producer or assigned to a particular station. In classical music there are two similar but distinct systems — the Hindustani or North Indian style and the Karnatak or South Indian style. For National Programmes of classical music the presentation is both in Hindi and English. The practice of announcements in two languages is also followed in programmes devoted to regional music, though in this case a lot more explanatory information on the content, mood and cultural context is required than in classical music.

Major problems however arise when it comes to literature, because without translation into the respective regional languages there would be little comprehension and no purpose would be served. Let us take the case of drama. For the National Programme a play from a regional language, let us suppose Assamese, is chosen. This is first translated into Hindi and the Hindi text together with the original in Assamese is sent to a selected station of each of the other language groups. There it undergoes a second translation into the regional language of that area. For instance, there are several stations broadcasting in Marathi, including Bombay, Pune (Poona) and Nagpur. The translation into Marathi will be entrusted to one of these stations and the Marathi production will be broadcast by all the stations of the Marathi group. Hindi being the national language, translators are available at all stations capable of translating from the regional language into Hindi and vice-versa. A well qualified person may not be available in Marathi; but in Bengal and Orissa, close neighbours of Assam, persons capable of direct translation from the original would be readily available, and in such cases there would be no need to go through the medium of a translation in Hindi.

By presenting national programmes of drama, features, poetry, short stories and the like, AIR has attempted to project one part of the country to the others and this has been one step in the direction of creating a national consciousness. A major symposium arranged by AIR in 1963 which was attended by literatteurs, educationists and others drawn from all the major language areas of India, focused attention on the problems of translation which are endemic to the cultural situation in this country.

Since 1950 AIR has been broadcasting programmes to teach Hindi, the national language, to listeners in non-Hindi speaking areas. The basic structure of these lessons, which are prepared in consultation with language experts, has undergone several changes over the years in the light of experience. Such lessons are broadcast three to five mornings a week from all non-Hindi speaking stations.

To deal with the developing schism between north and south, in which the fear of Hindi domination is a potent factor, AIR instituted the broadcast of south Indian language lessons from several north Indian stations. Thus Tamil, Telugu and Malayalam lessons are being broadcast from a number of stations in the north.

The growing demands of linguistic minorities for programmes in their own language have constituted a major problem for AIR. A broad guideline generally followed is to provide some programmes for a linguistic minority group if it consists of not less than five hundred thousand persons within the primary listening range of a station. Thus most stations are broadcasting in two or more languages other than English and Hindi. Bombay station, for example, is broadcasting in four languages, although it has only two channels on radio (apart from the Commercial Service which is a separate channel). The demand for separate programmes has spread to the dialects and at Patna, a single-channel station, programmes are being broadcast in three dialects of Hindi as a result of pressure. The situation is far more serious in the tribal areas of the north-east. Several stations are broadcasting in four or more dialects and the most extreme case, as we have seen, is found in Nagaland where Kohima, with a single channel, broadcasts in no less than thirteen dialects. Single channel broadcasting in several languages leads to duplication, fragmentation of transmission time, and in the end satisfies no one.

Broadcasting and Secularism

The Indian conception of secularism, which is an important pillar of the state, does not imply scepticism or indifference to religion but rather an attitude of equal respect for all religions. Another aspect of secularism is the replacement of traditional beliefs and practices by information based on scientific knowledge. The importance attached to science in modern India under the leadership of Jawaharlal Nehru is demonstrated by the adoption by Parliament in 1956 of a Science Policy Resolution to define the long-term objectives of the government's science policy, which include the propagation of scientific attitudes. These two aspects of secularism, equal respect for all religions and the fostering of a scientific attitude, have been pursued by AIR in various ways.

AIR's policy towards religion has been summed up in several statements in Parliament and in other fora. It has been clarified that AIR does not broadcast 'religious programmes as such'. However, coverage is given to public celebrations of festivals of all communities. This may involve relays from places of religious worship. For example, several stations of AIR relay the annual functions held at a famous Muslim shrine in Ajmer (Rajasthan) and these programmes are carried on special frequencies to facilitate relay by Pakistan. Special programmes of religious music are arranged on important religious occasions.

After the opening of the morning transmission of all AIR stations about half an hour is given to a programme of devotional music. These programmes are intended to represent all religious communities and are based on talent drawn from different parts of the country. According to the instructions the texts of the songs selected should be non-sectarian and advocate universal values. Thus a station in the south in its devotional programmes might possibly include a qawwali or chorus by a Muslim Sufi, a Sikh religious song, a Christian hymn sung by a tribal choral group and of course Hindu devotional songs based on both the north and south Indian classical systems.

In these ways it is claimed, broadcasting has attempted to make people aware of the beliefs and practices of different religions and to create an appreciation of and respect for all of them.

Nevertheless the-criticism persists that these so-called 'devotional and ethical' programmes have brought the Hindu religion in from the back door. The vast majority of the devotional songs broadcast are taken from Hinduism. Official enquiries showed that several stations in the south are setting apart particular days of the week for the exclusive broadcast of songs pertaining to different sects. A genuine problem for programmers is the paucity of hymns the text of which can be divorced from the creed of the religion which inspires them. Be that as it may, the fact remains that devotional programmes broadcast are predominantly Hindu in character.

An equally serious complaint is that essentially religious programmes are broadcast under the garb of culture. The biggest single complaint of this kind refers to the manner in which the two thousand, five hundredth anniversary of the Buddha was celebrated by the Government of India and no less by AIR. Special programmes went on for a whole year in 1956 and the performance has become a byword for over-kill. More recently there have been other examples. In 1974-75, Satya Narain Sinha, then Governor of Madhya Pradesh, who had earlier been Minister of Information and Broadcasting, suggested that AIR Bhopal should broadcast daily a recitation set to music of the epic poem Ramcharita Manas by the sixteenth century poet Tulsi Das. This work has been described as 'the most popular scripture among the common people of North India... as familiar to Hindus as the Bible is to the Christians.' Under orders of the Ministry this programme was broadcast and repeated over several years. When the SD after several years dropped the programme, the Governor complained to the Ministry. The Minister, determined to snub the DG who had argued that the programme was contrary to the secular policy of the Government, ordered that henceforth it should be broadcast from all North Indian stations! Moreover, if the Rama incarnation is propagated, Krishna cannot be permitted by his followers to be left far behind. So the Delhi station broadcasts on several mornings in the week a programme entitled Braj Madhuri, consisting of sayings of Lord Krishna with a commentary.

Propagation of the scientific attitude is being carried out through AIR and Doordarshan's non-formal educational programmes, which advocate farm, health, and other practices based on modern knowledge.

These programmes provide an antidote to superstition and dogma. The direct propagation of science is also taken up at two levels; at the elementary level in programmes directed to schools and in science programmes for the adult audience. Special provision has been made in Doordarshan Base Production Centres, to provide elementary scientific information relevant to villagers. In AIR science cells have been set up in thirteen stations to plan and produce science programmes for different audiences. At a sophisticated level new advances in science are discussed in national and other programmes addressed to highly educated audiences. In the prestigious annual Patel Lectures (named after Sardar Vallabhbhai Patel, India's first Minister for Information and Broadcasting after Independence), one in four of the series has been devoted to some aspect or other of science.

In 1973, one session of the Station Directors' Conference (almost an annual feature) was devoted to an analysis of AIR's science programmes and to framing policy guidelines on science programmes. The keynote address on 'Scientific Temper' was by Kalinga prize winner Dr Jagjit Singh. Science programmes, it was found, were compartmentalised; the scientific approach was not made part of the approach to every day life. Moreover, the publicity given to spectacular technological achievements tended to treat science itself as a form of magic. A comprehensive policy guidance note was drawn up but by and large it has remained a dead letter. The reason for this lies in the Indian conception of secularism which is taken as a negative concept implying non-interference in religious affairs, including superstitious rituals.

Clause 2 of the AIR Code, already discussed, does not permit 'attack on religion or communities'. A narrow or timid interpretation of the Code provides a sufficient handle for not criticising any aspect of religion; although the Constitution specifically empowers the state to limit the functions of religion if it endangers public order, health or morality. The positive aspects of secularism, such as a common civil code, and the duty to 'develop the scientific temper, humanism, and a spirit of enquiry and reform,' have found no place in broadcasting or in the educational system, for that matter.

Programme Schedules and Output: AIR

In the Home Services the percentage of time given to different programmes is as shown in Table 4.4.

Table 4.4

*Percentage of Time Given to Different Programmes
in the Home Services*

Categories	Percentage of Time
Classical music	12.8
Folk music	3.6
Light music	11.3
Film music	6.1
Western music	4.3
News & current affairs	24.6
Talks & discussions (including literary programmes)	6.8
Sport	4.8
Drama & features	3.7
Rural	6.3
Educational	3.7
Children's programmes	1.1
Women's programmes	1.6
Industrial programmes	1.2
Armed forces' programmes	1.6
Tribal	1.9
Publicity, announcements etc.	4.6

Note: The figures cited above vary slightly from those cited in U.L. Baruah, *This is All India Radio,* Publications Division, 1983, p. 46.
Source: Official estimates.

It will be observed that the total music output in the Home Services is approximately 38.1 per cent which is rather low in comparison with most broadcasting organisations. This is in part explained by the multiplicity of languages, which results in considerable duplication and the demands of different minority groups for satisfaction of their cultural and social requirements. In the commercial service approximately 70 per cent of the programme is music.

National and Regional Programmes

In the federal set-up of AIR, 70 per cent of the programmes are planned and produced at the stations; 24.8 per cent of time is given to news and current affairs and the remaining 5 per cent is taken up by National Programmes. These are network programmes carried by all stations such as a weekly 90-minutes recital of classical music, a weekly talk each in Hindi and English, monthly features and radio plays. There are some important networked annual events, among them the Patel Lectures in English and the Dr Rajendra Prasad Lectures in Hindi instituted in 1955 and in 1969 to commemorate independent India's first I & B Minister and President respectively. On the eve of Republic Day, 26 January, there is a national symposium of poets. One poem from each of the major languages adjudged to be the best amongst those broadcast in the previous year is selected. The author recites his poem in the original language which is followed by a verse translation in Hindi by a distinguished poet of this language who is specially commissioned for the purpose. The biggest single annual undertaking, the Sangeet Sammelan, is a series of classical music concerts which are organised over some two or three days at the four zonal centres — Delhi, Calcutta, Madras and Bombay — and half a dozen other stations selected in rotation. These are public concerts to which music-lovers are invited. Recordings of the concerts are subsequently broadcast on the national hook-up.

National and Regional News

The News Services Division is responsible for news bulletins and current affairs programmes. For the Home Services it produces 68 national news bulletins a day in 19 languages. In addition, 34 Regional News Units which are professionally responsible to the NSD put out 124 regional news bulletins daily in 22 languages and 34 dialects. There is a daily current affairs commentary in English, Hindi and Urdu, broadcast from Delhi at a peak listening time, one or two of which is relayed by most stations. Stations also put out their own regional language commentaries. There is a weekly discussion of half an hour's duration in English and Hindi on some current issue and most stations relay one or other of these. While Parliament is in session AIR covers the proceedings of each House in broadcasts of approximately 6.5 minutes each in English and Hindi. These reviews are broadcast simultaneously from Delhi and are relayed by stations; stations also schedule their own newsreels two or three times a week.

The distinction between national and regional bulletins is important. National bulletins are compiled in Delhi in English. They are then translated into the different languages of the region for which they are intended. In the case of Hindi the bulletin is prepared directly in the language of broadcast. National bulletins are broadcast on high power short-wave transmitters and now also via the satellite from Delhi and relayed on the regional medium-wave transmitters of the target area. Two sections, national and international news, are common. The third part varies from region to region, containing items of special interest to the area to which it is directed.

At the stations, receiving centres have been set up with special reception aerial systems to receive the news and to relay it on local transmitters.

In most of the languages in which national news bulletins are broadcast there are three newscasts a day each of ten minutes. These are between 7 AM and 9 AM in the morning, 12.30 PM and 2.20 PM and 6 PM and 8 PM. In Hindi and English there are twelve and thirteen bulletins a day respectively. The major bulletins in these languages follow the pattern of the others, that is morning, after-noon and evening. The morning and afternoon bulletins are of ten minutes' duration, the evening bulletin at 8.45 PM in Hindi.and 9 PM in English are of fifteen minutes. In both languages there is a five minute bulletin immediately after the transmission opens and another at the close of the day's transmission. Apart from these, between 10 AM and 1 PM and again from 3 to 6 PM there are news bulletins of 2.5 minutes each in Hindi and in English on the hour. Stations generally relay the major English news bulletins and they are all required to relay at least one major Hindi bulletin. Stations in the Hindi-speaking region relay all the Hindi bulletins which are broadcast during their transmission hours. The Commercial chan-nels relay the Hindi bulletins which fall within their transmission hours.

Regional bulletins of regional and local news are compiled at 34 stations by the Regional News Units. These are of five to ten minutes' duration and are broadcast generally twice a day, in the morning and in the evening transmission. The same news may be given out in two or more languages according to the number of lan-guages in which the station broadcasts.

The NSD also provides dictation speed bulletins which are consi-dered an important service for the benefit of small newspapers in the country. A daily twenty-minute bulletin in English and in Hindi is broadcast from Delhi. These are twenty-four hour cover-back bulletins for the benefit of small newspapers in the districts which are not served by news agency teleprinter services. In the case of

Kashmir the bulletins are translated into Urdu, thereby providing further assistance to local newspapers.

AIR subscribes to two English news agencies, Press Trust of India (PTI) and United News of India (UNI), and to two Hindi news agencies, Samachar Bharati and Hind Samachar. It employs over two hundred full-time correspondents, including seven foreign correspondents in Singapore, Cairo, Dubai, Dhaka, Colombo, Islamabad and Kathmandu. The last three posts were created at the end of 1985. It has also two hundred and seventeen part-time correspondents located in the districts whose principal task is to supply news for the regional news bulletins. A monitoring section located within the NSD in Delhi working round the clock keeps the editorial staff supplied with transcripts of newsheets of several foreign stations including BBC, VOA, Radio Australia, Pakistan and Bangladesh. The main office of the Director Monitoring Service AIR is located some 30 kms. south of Delhi and is connected by teleprinter with the NSD. The Monitoring Office covers the broadcasts of twenty-seven stations in fourteen languages and compiles daily and weekly reports for background information and analysis.

Current Affairs programmes are presented in several formats from Delhi in Hindi and English and are relayed by all stations. The Delhi commentaries follow the main Hindi and English news bulletins every night and on Sundays there is a half hour discussion. Newsreels in the two languages are a daily affair offered at prime time. This general pattern is duplicated at the stations with programmes in their respective languages.

When Parliament is in session there is a daily review of six minutes apiece in Hindi and English. These are relayed by all stations. The station in the state capital is responsible for daily reviews of the state legislature when in session.

Talks and Discussions

Talks and discussion programmes other than Current Affairs fill 6.8 per cent of AIR time. Reference has already been made to three important annual events, the Patel lectures (English), the Dr Rajendra Prasad lectures (Hindi), and the national symposium of poets on the eve of Republic Day. Talks and discussions, mainly in Hindi and the regional languages but also in English, cover a wide variety of subjects in the humanities and sciences, travelogues, book reviews, poetry recitation, short stories and the like.

A weekly National Talks programme in English and another in Hindi are relayed over the network. Distinguished personalities in various fields are invited to broadcast. However, in recent years, these talks have almost invariably been devoted to various aspects of government publicity.

Music

Music as mentioned occupies on the average 38.1 per cent of time. India has an ancient and continuous tradition of classical music which goes back to the early years of the Christian era. As noticed above, there are two schools, the Hindustani or North Indian School, and the Karnatak or South Indian style. During the British period, princely houses provided the patronage under which classical music flourished. Since 1947, AIR has done a great deal to fill the gap arising from the removal of the princes from the political scene. The weekly national programmes of music and the annual Sangeet Sammelan have done a great deal to popularise classical music.

Artists are approved for music broadcasts through a system of auditions by non-official committees at two levels. There is a preliminary screening at the stations. Those who pass, record a recital which is judged by a central committee, known as the Music Audition Board. The Board grades all artists into four categories: 'Top', 'A', 'B (High)' and 'B'. The justification for a central authority is that a national standard for classical artists is necessary since classical music is an art form common to the country as a whole.

India also has a rich and varied tradition of devotional, light and folk music. In these programmes the language of the text plays an important part and the artists are generally confined to broadcasts from their own regional or language stations. But national programmes are also organised in these forms to give each linguistic area an idea of what is happening in others.

A special word is necessary about Indian film music which from the point of view of popularity may be described as the country's version of pop. Film music comprises lyrics, mainly love songs, set to syncopated rhythms with a good deal of what is known as 'orchestration'. The majority of Indian films being in Hindi, most film songs are also in Hindi. The songs of other Indian language films tend to approximate to the Hindi model. During the fifties AIR banned film music on the ground that it was vulgar, both musically and in respect of the texts of the lyrics. But film music was and is very popular especially with audiences below the age of thirty and the Commercial Service of Radio Ceylon captured listeners by beaming programmes of film music to India. As a result, AIR's policy changed. The light programme channel, Vividh Bharati, started in 1957 and came to carry film music for 90 per cent of its time and, on its successor, the Commercial Channel, some 70 per cent of the music consists of film music. On the regional channels it occupies only 6 per cent.

An experiment of interest is the setting up in 1952 of an Indian orchestra in Delhi known as the National Orchestra or Vadya Vrinda. Indian music is basically melodic and the Western concepts of harmonisation and orchestration are foreign to it. This orchestra with Ravi Shankar as conductor and consisting mainly of Indian instruments was constituted to experiment in a new dimension for traditional music. After Ravi Shankar resigned from AIR in the late fifties, a number of other distinguished Indian musicians functioned as its conductor. In 1977 a second National Orchestra was set up at the Madras Station.

Western music which occupies 1 per cent of the time given to music is broadcast from about a dozen stations. Pop music is popular with the younger urban set and classical music has its votaries among the older generation. While most of the programmes are based on gramophone records there are a number of performing artists, a few chamber music ensembles, and symphony orchestras in the four metropolitan centres.

Drama and Features

Drama occupies 3.7 per cent of broadcast time and is broadcast from most stations, in the respective regional languages and in some of the major dialects. Once a month there is a national programme play chosen from the best of the regional languages productions. The script in the original language together with a translation in Hindi is circulated to the major stations of each language zone, about fifteen of them. It is then translated into the regional language and the play in each of the languages is broadcast by each station simultaneously on an agreed date. While in certain cases translation has to be through the medium of Hindi, in others translators can be found who can work directly from the original which is of course preferable.

There is a powerful theatre movement in several parts of India, the foremost playwrights being Badal Sircar (Bengali), Vijay Tendulkar (Marathi), Girish Karnad (Kannada), and Mohan Rakesh (Hindi), who died in 1972 at the age of 47. Some playwrights have also distinguished themselves as producers and actors. The works of these have marginally affected the field of radio drama. The ordinary run of radio plays is not of a high standard. The rate of payment is poor and there is little scope for their utilisation elsewhere. There have been some exceptions. One such was *Tumhare Ghum Mere Hain* (Your Woes Are Mine) written by the Delhi playwright Reoti Sharan Sharma, who has devoted himself specifically to the radio play. This play (scheduled in the National Programme in 1979, called off under Janata government orders at the last minute) was subsequently presented on the Delhi stage and is now being made into a film. It is a touching story of the problems faced by an inter-caste married couple — Brahmin woman and Harijan husband. Another radio play entitled *Harud* (Autumn) written originally in Kashmiri by Dr Shankar Raina was put on the boards in Hindi in Delhi, awarded a prize and then staged in several foreign countries.

Included within the drama output is the dramatised radio documentary which is a popular form in India. It has been used to publicise important national development projects, to highlight historical events and also, though to a lesser extent, as a format for investigative reporting. Feature writers and producers have, however, done little to experiment with new forms for presentation.

Educational Broadcasts

At present educational programmes occupy 3.7 per cent of the total broadcast time. Seventy-one stations originate programmes for school children. Programmes for schools were started by stations under the Indian Broadcasting Company. They have been a regular feature since AIR came into operation. At the initial stage the broadcasts were intended for students at the secondary school level and the bulk of programmes are still directed to such audiences. There has since been an extension both at the upper and lower ends. Programmes in support of University Correspondence Courses at the degree level were introduced in Delhi more than a decade ago. These programmes are re-broadcast from the Jaipur (Rajasthan) and Madras stations. A large number of students in these states are interested in obtaining Delhi University degrees. In more recent years similar educational broadcasts have been introduced at Jalandhar station and at Tiruchirapalli (Tamil Nadu) where the Panjab and Madurai Universities have instituted correspondence courses at degree level. At the lower end, broadcasts for primary schools were introduced first in the state of Maharashtra and are now being originated from radio stations in six other states. These programmes are generally broadcast five days in a week during term time. Many of these stations broadcast programmes for school teachers during the vacations.

Educational programmes are planned and produced at stations in their respective languages to suit their own particular needs. There is a School Broadcast Panel which advises on the schedules on which the State Education Departments are represented. Programmes are planned and produced as in-school listening and a chart giving the scheduled programmes and an explanatory booklet are sent to the registered schools. The listening end is the responsibility of the education department and the schools. AIR has advised from time to time on technical matters, but funds and organisation have to be provided by the educational authorities. Their general failure to do so has been the weakness of educational broadcasting in India for the past forty years. Only a small percentage of schools in a few states, such as Maharashtra, Tamil Nadu and Kashmir, have made adequate arrangements for listening under proper supervision.

One of the arguments put forward by the educational authorities has been that the school timetable is over-burdened as it is and that it is impossible to find a place for radio lessons. It was to get over this difficulty that AIR recently introduced programmes for primary classes in the belief that there would be more time and flexibility at this stage of education. This move has been welcomed in certain quarters.

In the case of broadcasts in support of correspondence courses AIR Stations plan the programmes in consultation with the University authorities. Listening is on an individual basis. The demand by students for refresher courses, particularly before examinations indicate that the programmes are serving a purpose if a limited one.

The need for far greater cooperation between programme producers, educational authorities and teachers is generally recognised. The setting up of Educational Broadcast Councils to effect such coordination was proposed by the Verghese Working Group which referred to the Council established in West Bengal. In fact the West Bengal

Educational Broadcast Council has existed only on paper and has never met in the last two decades.

Sport

Sport has come to occupy an increasingly important place in AIR programmes in recent years and now occupies 4.8 per cent of the time. Cricket for example is enormously popular and ball by ball commentaries of Test and other important matches over five days have drawn very large audiences since the earliest days of radio. But apart from commentaries on important tournaments in cricket, hockey and football, little time is devoted to sport in the normal schedule. Since 1974 a daily sports service of 1 hour and 45 minutes has been scheduled which covers important games in different parts of the country and there is a daily sports news bulletin of five minutes each in Hindi and English at 8.00 PM which is relayed by all stations. There is also a weekly sports newsreel. Test cricket, international hockey and tennis, Olympic, Asian and Commonwealth Games are all covered within the financial resources available to the organisation. It can happen that the normal schedules, including news bulletins otherwise considered sacrosanct, are disrupted in the interest of sports coverage, though some murmurs of protest from the listening public have begun to be heard on this score.

Other Programmes

Industrial programmes (1.4 per cent) are broadcast by fifteen stations in highly industrialised areas. They are informational in content. There are Industrial Advisory Committees at these stations which advise on the nature and content of their programmes.

The 2.4 per cent of time that is given to publicity refers to announcements of public interest. For example, posts advertised by the Union and State Public Service Commissions, missing persons, announcements regarding public health and so on fall under this category.

AIR's programmes for Children and Women follow lines common to most broadcasting organisations. AIR plans special programmes for women in the rural areas and for working women.

Programmes for the Armed Forces consist largely of light music and letters from home especially for those stationed in the border areas and of information on service matters.

The Commercial Service

The Commercial Service, as its predecessor Vividh Bharati, was conceived as an all-India service, a national pre-recorded programme radiated from different centres.

A code for Commercial Advertising for AIR was introduced in 1967 when the service started. Commercials are limited to 10 per cent of transmission time and the Code prohibits advertising of tobacco, liquor and gambling, including betting on horse-racing and other sports. Each commercial broadcast centre functions under a Station Director, who is responsible to the Deputy Director-General (Commercial) in New Delhi.

The Commercial Service is currently broadcast from some twenty-nine centres and reaches approximately 15 per cent of the population. The duration of the programme varies from twelve to fourteen hours a day. Its income is a little more than 10 per cent of the annual budget of AIR.

The language of presentation continued for several years to be exclusively Hindi, and commercials were centralised in Bombay under a Central Sales Unit. Thus if an advertiser in Cuttack for instance desired to book a spot on the local commercial channel he had to deal with the Central Sales Unit in Bombay which approved and finalised the transaction. The procedure was cumbersome and anyway advertising through the medium of Hindi and English was not considered of much use to the small entrepreneur interested in the local market.

To get over these difficulties there has been some decentralisation in the procedure for selling time. While booking of time is still mainly done at Bombay the commercial broadcast centres have been permitted to deal directly with advertisers for a small part of the total time available. This may vary between 10 and 20 per cent. In a total trasmission of 12 hours the total time available would be 1 hour 12 minutes and of this between 6 and 14 minutes could be sold directly by the centre while bookings for the balance would be made by the Central Sales Unit in Bombay.

Commercial broadcasting centres have also been made responsible for the daily origination of a programme in the regional language of a duration ranging from 30 to 50 minutes. Advertisements in the regional language are accepted. A 15 per cent rebate is offered to advertisers of handicrafts and products of small-scale industries.

These measures have helped the smaller centres to sell the time available on their respective channels.

Advertising material is permitted at the beginning and end of a programme. The sale of time for spot commercials is divided into three categories: Super A, A and C. Spots of 15 seconds, 30 seconds and 60 seconds are acceptable. There are four separate rates, the highest being applicable to Bombay, the second highest to Calcutta, the third to Delhi, and the lowest rate is applied at Madras and all other centres. Sponsored programmes are accepted at all centres. The rate for sponsored programmes is approximately twice the A time rate.

Advertising material may also be channelled through advertising agencies which are accredited to AIR. Accreditation of an agency is based on a variety of factors, including capital investment, annual turnoyer etc. There are three categories of accredited agencies: accredited, recognised and registered. Agencies of the first two categories are entitled to 15 per cent commission. Accredited agencies also get credit of forty days which commences on the first of the month following the broadcast of spots or sponsored programmes. Registered agencies receive 10 per cent commission.

An internal committee of officials on which a representative of the Ministry of Finance is included considers applications from advertising agents for accreditation. Advertising rates are reviewed from time to time in AIR headquarters and in the Ministry. Rates have been revised several times since the Commercial Service came into operation. The last occasion was in 1975.

Yuv Vani: The Voice of Youth

Yuv Vani consists of several different types of programmes. There are the many varieties of light, including pop, and classical music. There is also a youth choir. *Campus News,* which provides investigative reporting under a programme entitled *The Roving Microphone,* has enquired into a number of youth problems. One programme which also attracts considerable interest among grown-ups is *Firing Line.* Distinguished politicians, academics, writers, artists and senior managers are put through a hard-hitting question and answer session. Sports and literary programmes are also provided.

Once a week a selected programme from Yuv Vani is presented on the main channel of Delhi station so that it can reach a wider audience. A signal service rendered by Yuv Vani has been to discover youngsters in very humble positions who have become well-known and have been able to improve their lot in life. A high-school boy working in a laundry has been able to get on to a newspaper because of his capacity to write and another, who sells betel leaves on the pavement, is being increasingly invited by literary organisations to participate in their poetry symposia. (In India, symposia where poets recite their verses known as *mushairas* or *kavi samellans*, attract huge crowds and are important occasions in our cultural life.)

Yuv Vani in Delhi is presented in Hindi and English. It runs for some six and a half hours a day. University broadcasts in support of correspondence courses are also carried on this channel. Yuv Vani functions under the Station Director. The Programme Executives and Producers are under thirty years of age.

Some important centres such as Bombay and Madras do not, at present, have separate Yuv Vani channels. But most stations are providing programme times between fourteen hours and thirty minutes in a week on their channels for Yuv Vani, planned and presented on the same lines as the Delhi output.

External Services: AIR

Currently AIR broadcasts in its External Services for a total of some 56 hours a day in twenty-five languages including English. There are sixteen foreign languages and eight Indian languages. The major services are the General Overseas Service in English for ten hours, and the Urdu Service for twelve hours. The former is targeted to Asia, Australia, New Zealand, East, West and North Africa, Britain and Western Europe, and the latter to Pakistan. The Urdu Service also commands considerable listening in India. The other services are in Arabic, Baluchi, Bengali, Burmese, Cantonese, Dari, French, Gujarati, Hindi, Indonesian, Konkani, Mandarin, Nepali, Persian, Punjabi, Pushto, Russian, Sindhi, Sinhala, Swahili, Thai and Tibetan.

The two major services, the General Overseas Service in English and the Urdu Service, are put on four separate transmitters each. With the exception of the Baluchi and Thai services, which are for thirty minutes each, the other services vary from one to three hours daily and are put out in two transmissions. The core of each transmission is a news bulletin of ten minutes' duration, a review of the

Indian press and a commentary of five minutes duration on current affairs. Spoken word programmes on various aspects of Indian life, industrial development and exports and information of interest to tourists are among the many subjects which figure in the schedules. Music is exclusively Indian music in the English and the Indian language services. Indian music and especially film music is popular in many countries in Europe, in the Arab world and Afghanistan and in South-East Asia. In the foreign language services, the music of the region to which the service is directed is also included.

Judging from listeners' letters, several of the services are popular, particularly in the neighbouring countries such as Pakistan, Afghanistan, Bangladesh, Burma and Nepal. The major difficulty in services directed to more distant parts of the world is the inadequacy in transmitter capacity. Currently, the most powerful short-wave transmitters in AIR are of 250 kilowatt strength and the number of such transmitters is extremely limited. Attempts to reduce the number of languages and to devote more of the available resources to what may be considered the important services have not met with success. This is one point on which the Ministry of External Affairs has had the last word.

Doordarshan : Programme Schedules and Output

The Audience Research Unit of the Doordarshan Directorate has compiled some useful figures on the composition of Doordarshan's programmes from various points of view.

This compilation gives the breakdown, format-wise, of the programmes of six of the main kendras. (See Appendix Table 4A.)

The average percentage of light entertainment comes to 29 per cent. (I include in this category serials/plays/skits/feature films/ Chitrahaar*). The figures for Delhi and Bombay are higher than the average and for Calcutta and Madras below it.

The average for news is 12 per cent and does not vary appreciably, except in the case of Madras, where it is only 9 per cent. This is because of the Tamil Nadu Government's objection to the relay of Hindi bulletins.

The compilation gives the languagewise composition of the

---

*Chitrahaar is an extremely popular programme consisting of a series of song-and-dance sequences from Hindi films.

six kendras. (See Appendix Table 4B.) Except in the case of Madras the largest percentage of programmes is in Hindi, averaging 39 per cent. Even in Calcutta Hindi comes first with 34 per cent. Regional language programmes get approximately 24 per cent, except in the case of Madras where Tamil gets pride of place with 40 per cent. English gets 28 per cent of the average and falls at the lowest to 21 per cent in the case of Jalandhar. Other Indian languages get 3 per cent, excluding Urdu which gets 2 per cent, mainly no doubt because of the Srinagar kendra in Kashmir, where the national language is Urdu. (Kashmir, unlike the other states has both a regional language and a national language.)

The official reference gives the composition by language and format of three sample satellite and post-SITE centres. (See Appendix Tables 4C and 4D.)

A comparison with the figures for the main centres shows that the differences between them are negligible, although these centres are supposed to cater to rural audiences. More significant than the format composition is that in respect of language. While the percentage of programmes in Hindi is 4 per cent higher, in the case of English it is 10 per cent higher than in the main centres. In the post-SITE centre at Hyderabad, the dominant language is English, with 37 per cent of programming. Hindi gets first place at the centres at Delhi and Nagpur; Hindi is the regional language of Delhi, while Nagpur is situated in a bi-lingual area where Hindi and Marathi are the regional languages. The regional languages, namely Tamil from Hyderabad and Marathi at Nagpur, get 25 per cent and 27 per cent respectively.

The National Programme is responsible for these aberrations as it takes up approximately two hours of prime time every evening, and for the majority of centres that is all the telecasting they do. The official compilation gives the composition of the National Programme by format. (See Appendix Table 4E.)

We see that 27 per cent of programmes are light entertainment, and 32 per cent is news. The high percentage of news is one reason why the non-Congress state governments have objected to it. A table in the official compilation (4.3, not reproduced here) shows that 54 per cent of the National Programme is produced in Delhi. A mere 3 per cent is produced in Bombay and the contribution of the other kendras is negligible. 23 per cent is provided by 'outside sources in India' (this presumably means programmes by Indian sponsors) and no less than 10 per cent consists of imported programmes.

The language-wise composition is as follows: Hindi gets 46 per cent, English 44 per cent, Urdu 2 per cent, Punjabi 1 per cent and all the other Indian languages put together get 1 per cent. Instrumental music and dance make up the balance. (See Table 4.1 of the Doordarshan Directorate's Audience Research Unit's compilation.)

Considering there was no preparation, it is surprising how quickly Doordarshan has adapted to colour. 99 per cent of the National Programme is produced in colour. Delhi and Bombay provide 98 per cent of programmes in colour. The average production in colour is 83 per cent. Colour production in Madras is lowest, 52 per cent.

The scene sketched above has emerged since August 1982. Prior to that there was no network service; programmes were produced at the kendras for their local audiences in their own languages. Then came the satellite link and the special plan with its array of transmitters sans studios and the relay of the National Programme. Doordarshan was transformed into a centralised system. In 1983 the door was opened to sponsored programmes and a staid government medium supposedly dedicated to social development, has become an instrument for purveying light entertainment, soap opera and consumerism. Almost the only category of programmes which continues untouched is news and government publicity, heavy-handed and unimaginative. One plus-point that the box has gained from commercials is sport, national and international, with coverage of athletics, hockey, tennis and the ubiquitous cricket with its ball-to-ball commentaries spreading over five days. Commercial advertising is statutorily restricted to 10 per cent of the transmission time. A precise analysis would tend to show that spots are exceeding this limit. In reply to the Ministry's demands for grants in the Lok Sabha on 25 April 1986, the Minister for Information and Broadcasting said that 'the time allotted for advertisements on Doordarshan would stand frozen at 5 per cent of the total transmission and for sponsored programmes at 11 per cent.' The figures are at variance with what we have cited. However, the Minister's language is ambiguous. What is the meaning of 'would stand frozen at'? The most obvious interpretation is that advertisements/sponsored programmes occupy 5 per cent and 11 per cent respectively and this will continue. But if that were the case, where was the need for this figurative language? Certainly the Ministry of Information and Broadcasting, in its pursuit of money, has no respect for artistic integrity or sensitivity. Spots break into the few programmes of high aesthetic value that the service attempts. The Ministry's reports to parliament in recent years have spoken of Doordarshan's Commercial Service. This would ordinarily give the impression that this is one of at least two channels. However, two channels exist only at Delhi and Bombay and commercials are evident on both. It would be more correct to speak of the commercialisation of Doordarshan's entire service.

News and Current Affairs

There are daily newscasts in Hindi and English of twenty minutes each in the National Programme, and again news headlines at the close of the programme. Each of the main kendras telecasts a bulletin in the regional language or languages.

Doordarshan does not have its own central organisation for news collection and dissemination and depends for this on AIR. AIR's pool copy is received by Doordarshan and the TV news is based on it. TV news, therefore is largely confined to reading out radio news bulletins with a few visuals thrown in. Recently Doordarshan entered into a contract with a private agency sponsored by a business house, for the supply of TV news. Doordarshan has about a hundred stringers in different parts of the country and the visual coverage provided by them is entirely on film. It accounts for a very small percentage of the news carried by the service

On November 1984, Doordarshan joined the Asia Vision News exchange programme organised by ABU. This enables Doordarshan both to receive TV news from some other Asian countries and to send news to them. In addition, Doordarshan subscribes to two major news agencies, Visnews and Transtel.

There are daily reports of Parliament when it is in session, and of proceedings of state legislatures wherever there is a kendra. All these are presented as straight readings of scripts by a speaker on the screen. Current affairs programmes take the form of discussions among experts and interviews with prominent personalities. The common man or woman hardly ever figures.

Farm, Health and Family Welfare Programmes

Doordarshan kendras broadcast programmes for rural audiences two or three times a week consisting of agricultural information built around visuals. Programmes are planned in consultation with departments of agriculture on animal husbandry and the like. Programmes on village crafts, nutrition, health and family welfare are also regular features. We have already noted in our discussion of SITE that Doordarshan farm programmes have little advice to offer on local requirements. TV seems to be addressing itself to affluent farmers.

Educational Programmes

Doordarshan Delhi, has been telecasting syllabus-oriented programmes for Higher Secondary schools since 1961. These telecasts are planned jointly with the education department of the Delhi Administration and are produced by Doordarshan. Three twenty-minute programmes are telecast each morning on five days a week and repeated in the afternoon for the benefit of the second shift. The subjects covered are the English language, physics, chemistry, biology, geography and mathematics.

In 1975, Doordarshan introduced two twenty-minute programmes per week for primary school children. These programmes are of a general nature and are not tied to a syllabus. One programme a week is telecast for teachers with suggestions for the proper utilisation of the medium for education. Responsibility for organising the television reception in schools rests with the education authorities.

The Delhi pattern is also followed in Bombay and these are the only two centres which provide programmes for in-school viewing. The total number of TV sets in schools in Delhi and Bombay is 543 (see the audience research compilation, p. 59). Non-formal education programmes for small children are telecast from Madras and Srinagar, twice weekly by the former and once a week by the latter.

To date there has been only one survey of the utilisation of Delhi's telecasts for schools, conducted by AIR's Audience Research Unit in the early seventies. The report was not encouraging. In nearly 50 per cent of the schools visited the sets were not being used, either because they were out of order, the key was not to be found, or for some other reason. Viewing conditions were unsatisfactory. For example, in several cases the room could not be appropriately darkened because there were no curtains.

In short, although school telecasts are a joint undertaking by the education and Doordarshan authorities, the general picture is not very different from that which we find in radio. Teachers, it appears, feel threatened by the media and are not prepared to let them into the school system.

University Grants Commission Programmes on Higher Education

When satellite INSAT IB became operative, time was available for TV programmes, but no preparation had been made for its utilisation. The UGC made a bid and was successful in acquiring two slots of 45 minutes each at 1245 and 1645 hours every day, except Saturdays, Sundays and holidays. The UGC programme for higher education, as it is billed, is entirely in English and is available for other kendras as they choose. The content is made up mostly of video recordings obtained from Britain's Open University, with the balance being contributed by programmes produced at a few university centres where departments of mass communication have been hurriedly set up in the last three years. The UGC has been lavish in giving funds to help establish such departments, one condition being that they will contribute items for its TV programmes. Short of trained staff to man their faculties, these departments have been hard put to meet their assigned quotas. What has resulted is a repetition of the classroom lecture, with microphone and camera added. By far the largest number of programmes is on science. Who views these programmes? The UGC has not bothered to find out. Indeed, on the face of it, the timings would appear unsuitable. Students would normally be at their classes for the first slot. Science students would be doing their practicals when the repeat programme comes on the box at 1645 hours and Arts students might just be back from college or on the playing fields. Does the UGC really care? They have established their claim to the slots and a further expansion of their empire has been won.

Science Programmes

Science units have been set up at TV centres which are responsible for producing programmes on everyday science. These programmes are designed to fit into the schedule of different programme categories, such as programmes for rural folk, school children and the like. Outside producers have been commissioned from time to time to produce programmes on specified topics.

Sport

As in other countries, TV coverage of sporting events has been very popular in India. Since the Asian Games and with the introduction of sponsorship, Doordarshan has taken some notable initiatives. In 1984, for the Olympic Games held in Los Angeles, Doordarshan arranged, for the first time, live telecasts of the opening and closing ceremonies. All the hockey matches played by India were telecast live. In addition, capsules of one hundred minutes brought to Indian viewers the outstanding events of the day. Among other noteworthy international events now covered are Wimbledon Finals, the US Open Finals, Uber Cup and Thomas Badminton Finals, South Asian Federation Games, and Test cricket. All major national sports events are covered.

The quality of Doordarshan's coverage is commonly regarded as poor. Commentators talk endlessly, as if they were engaged on a commentary for radio. Most of the comment is irrelevant. The camera often misses the important point and there are no facilities for playback at slow speed.

Documentaries

Some of the deficiencies in Doordarshan visual coverage are made good by documentaries which make up 7 per cent of the output of national programmes. TV camera teams have been sent out to cover floods, which are something of an annual feature in Indian life, cyclones, such as the one which devastated Andhra Pradesh in 1978, important fairs and pilgrimages in different parts of the country.

There is now one company, known as TV News Features (TVNF) which has its own production facilities in New Delhi and with whom Doordarshan has a contract for the supply of science films and news features. One programme a month on science and one documentary on an aspect of development are being supplied by this firm to the different television centres. Silent edit prints are sent to the centres with a commentary, script and timing sheets in English to enable the producers to put over the programme in the local language.

Music and Dance

In music, Doordarshan follows the grading and the fee structure of,

AIR. Thus, only those artists who have been approved by AIR's audition boards are invited by Doordarshan. But Doordarshan can decide which AIR artists will be chosen for TV programmes according to its requirements, whereas AIR is virtually under compulsion to book artists approved by the audition boards. Doordarshan centres are under no such obligation.

For dance performances Doordarshan tends to confine itself to artists of the different classical and folk forms who have already established themselves. There is, so far, no formal system with independent experts to approve and grade artists.

Feature Films

It is commonly accepted in India that the prime consideration in investing in a TV set is to enable all members of the household to watch the feature films telecast by all Doordarshan centres. The main centres show one Hindi film a week on Sundays. In addition, there are two other films a week — in English or in any regional language, or film classics. Doordarshan centres thus present three films a week. The SITE continuity centres telecast one film a week.

Television centres have to negotiate with the film distributors for the right to screen a film. A board with a non-official majority has been set up in Bombay which approves films for telecast. Only films certified for universal exhibition are considered by the board.

Government has laid down rates which Doordarshan may offer to a distributor depending on the date of release of a film. These rates are for five categories of films : films up to three years old; films more than three years, but not more than five years old; films between five and seven years vintage; films between seven and ten years; and films released over ten years ago.

It may be said straightaway that hardly any film released within the last three years is ever broadcast on television since it takes about five years for a good film to complete the round of cinemas on the all-India circuit. Until a film has completed this run the distributors are not prepared to allow it to be shown on TV for fear it will affect the box office. Occasionally a distributor who feels that a particular film will not be a draw in a particular area will be prepared to release it for screening on TV at the centre concerned. This happened in the case of a new-wave Hindi film, *Garam Hawa*, directed by the distinguished young Bombay Director, M.S. Sathyu. The film deals with tensions created within a Muslim family which finds itself more and more isolated because of the situation prevailing in India shortly after partition. Due to the setting in Agra and the nature of the problem dealt with, the distributor was of the opinion that it would be a box office success in northern India but would not have much appeal in Calcutta. So he was prepared to release it for screening by the Calcutta centre, but not for Delhi.

Another problem which has arisen in the screening of feature films concerns the terms of the contract entered into between producers and distributors. The fact is that until recently the contract made no specific reference to TV. The distributors contended that in the absence of any clause to the contrary the rights of distribution acquired by them were absolute and included distribution not only in cinemas but also on TV. Producers have been reluctant to take the distributors to court or to antagonise them in any way because of the financial stranglehold which the distributors exercise on the whole film industry. However, producers are becoming more aware of their rights. As Doordarshan expands, film screening rights on TV will become an important bargaining counter in the hands of producers.

Despite the complaints that films screened by Doordarshan are of poor quality and out of date, the fact remains that feature films command the largest TV audiences. Apart from screening whole films, Doordarshan centres present at least one weekly programme of half an hour's duration composed of song-and-dance sequences from films. Chitrahaar (literally a garland of pictures), Delhi's Doordarshan programme in this genre, is extremely popular. Film distributors are anxious to get a couple of song-and-dance sequences included in Chitrahaar because of the publicity it gives the films which may be running in the city. Interviews with film stars is another type of programme which is a popular weekly feature on Doordarshan.

Many critics have been distressed by the manner in which the Indian film world has been eroding the basic objective of television as an instrument for social education. While Indian films are admittedly of a high technical quality and earn valuable foreign exchange, the vast majority are escapist and uphold value systems which are socially conservative, if not downright reactionary. Indian films thus pose a major threat to Doordarshan, already shackled as it is by out-moded technology and indecision on fundamental issues.

TV Films

Doordarshan has in the last few years made an attempt to commission feature films by eminent film makers. The first such film was by Satyajit Ray, based on a story by the famous Hindi novelist Prem Chand, entitled *Sadgati*. It was telecast in black and white and was a powerful satire on caste. Since then, other distinguished directors have produced films for Doordarshan. The special TV films have not yet had time to make a major impact, since the number telecast so far has been small.

Serials

Family serials came into their own in the year 1984-85. At least six were on at the same time, all sponsored, and were raking in to government coffers half the total commercial revenues of Doordarshan. Hindi feature films and film-based programmes such as Chitrahar, hitherto believed to be the most popular programmes were left far behind. This is the finding of the Operations Research Group (Baroda) which has been conducting continuous studies on Doordarshan's commercial operations. The most popular of the Hindi serials has undoubtedly been *Hum Log* which wound up in December 1985, after 256 episodes. Many distinguished film directors and actors have made their way into the family serials and some new actors and actresses have emerged.

The serials have their drawbacks. Sentimentality, ham acting and all the other vulgarities associated with Indian cinema, are to be found here. And there are recurring reports of corruption in the acceptance of serials.

A few fall into a different category. They are not family soap opera serials but serious novels or plays which have been serialised, such as Bhisham Sahni's novel, *Basanti. Darpan*, presents on Sunday afternoons a series of dramatised versions of short stories by well known authors. These are some of the oases in Doordarshan's desert of entertainment.

SITE Continuity Programmes

The general pattern of SITE continuity programmes follows the model which was operative during the experiment. There is, however, one difference. The morning programme for in-school viewing under the supervision of a teacher has been discontinued. The programme content has been altered and is now of a general nature. The reason for this change is that during SITE, the base production centres were preparing a programme of one visual with two audio channels which was shared by two neighbouring clusters. The SITE villages took the audio channel appropriate to their own language from the satellite, but with terrestrial transmitters this arrangement cannot function. The base production centres have to produce a separate complete package for each transmitter and facilities of the three base production centres have been increased only marginally.

The INSAT service has been introduced in six states, viz Andhra Pradesh, Bihar, Gujarat, Maharashtra, Orissa and Uttar Pradesh. Two thousand direct reception sets and two thousand VHF sets for community viewing in the villages of these states are expected to be in operation by April 1986. About half this number are functioning now.

APPENDIX

Table 4A

Composition of Programmes by Format (August 1985)

(Figures in percentages)

Format	Delhi*	Bombay*	Calcutta	Madras	Jalandhar	Lucknow	Total
			MAIN KENDRAS				
Serial/Play/Skit	17	18	14	14	16	17	16
Spoken Word items	16	35	13	26	14	20	21
News	12	10	14	9	12	12	12
Music Vocal/Instrumental	11	3	9	7	11	11	9
Feature Film/Chitrahaar	10	11	20	16	10	14	13
Documentary	3	3	4	5	6	4	5
Sports	9	9	14	10	11	13	11
Demonstration/TV Report/Recitation	4	2	4	3	9	3	4
Quiz	3	2	2	2	4	3	3
Dance	2	1	2	3	2	2	2
Slide/Filler/Highlight/							
Announcement/Commercial	4	6	4	5	5	2	4
TOTAL:	288 hrs. 52 mts.	277 hrs. 18 mts.	210 hrs. 5 mts.	234 hrs. 18 mts	244 hrs. 23 mts.	230 hrs. 21 mts.	1483 hrs. 37 mts.

Note: * Including Channel II.

Source: Doordarshan Directorate, *Audience Research Unit Compilation*, p. 39.

Table 4B

Composition of Programmes by Language (August 1985)

(Figures in percentages)

Language	MAIN KENDRAS						
	Delhi*	Bombay*	Calcutta	Madras	Jalandhar	Lucknow	Total
English	32	30	30	23	21	30	28
Hindi	51	30	34	24	41	53	39
Urdu	2	1	1	1	4	4	2
Marathi	—	25	—	—	—	—	5
Bengali	—	—	25	—	—	—	4
Tamil	—	—	—	40	—	—	6
Punjabi	5	—	—	—	24	7	5
Other Indian languages	—	6	2	2	2	—	3
Foreign languages	—	—	—	1	—	—	—
No-language Programme							
— Instrumental Music	4	1	2	2	2	2	2
— Dance	2	1	2	3	2	2	2
Slide/Filler/Highlight/ Announcement/Commercial	4	6	4	4	4	2	4
TOTAL:	288 hrs. 52 mts.	277 hrs. 18 mts.	210 hrs. 5 mts.	234 hrs. 18 mts.	244 hrs. 23 mts.	230 hrs. 21 mts.	1483 hrs. 37 mts.

Note: * Including Channel II.
Source: Doordarshan Directorate, Audience Research Unit Compilation, p. 38.

Table 4C

Composition of Programmes by Language (August 1985)

(Figures in percentages)

Language	POST-SITE/INSAT KENDRAS			
	UDK Delhi	*Hyderabad*	*Nagpur*	*Total*
English	31	37	30	34·
Hindi	55	26	33	38
Urdu	3	2	2	2
Marathi	—	—	27	5
Tamil	—	25	—	11
Other Indian languages	3	2	1	2
No-language Programme				
— Instrumental	3	2	3	3
— Dance	2	2	3	2
Slide/Filler/Highlight/ Commercial/Announcement	3	4	1	3
TOTAL:	225 hrs. 22 mts.	261 hrs. 43 mts.	104 hrs. 47 mts.	591 hrs. 52 mts.

Source: Doordarshan Directorate, *Audience Research Unit Compilation*, p. 42.

Table 4D

Composition of Programmes by Format (August 1985)

(Figures in percentages)

Format	POST-SITE/ INSAT KENDRAS			
	UDK Delhi	*Hyderabad*	*Nagpur*	**Total**
Serial/Play/Skit	19	15	17	17
Spoken Word items	17	9	19	14
News	14	11	21	14
Music Vocal/Instrumental	9	7	13	9
Feature Film/Chitrahaar	12	14	8	12
Documentary	6	15	8	10
Sports	10	9	1	8
Demonstration/TV Report/ Recitation	5	12	5	8
Quiz	3	2	4	3
Dance	2	2	3	2
Slide/Filler/Highlight/ Announcement/Commercial	3	4	1	3
TOTAL:	225 hrs. 22 mts.	261 hrs. 43 mts.	104 hrs. 47 mts.	591 hrs. 52 mts.

Source: Doordarshan Directorate, *Audience Research Unit Compilation*, p. 43.

Table 4E

Composition of National Programmes by Format (August 1985)

(*Figures in percentages*)

Format	Duration
Serial/Play/Skit	22
Spoken word items	13
News	32
Music Vocal/Instrumental	7
Feature Film/Chitrahaar	5
Documentary	7
Sports	2
Demonstration/TV Report/Recitation	5
Quiz	5
Dance	2
TOTAL:	70 hrs. 55 mts.

Source: Doordarshan Directorate, *Audience Research Unit Compilation*, p. 51.

Enquiries into Broadcasting 5

A fter Independence the Government set up a number of commissions or high-powered committees to examine the organisation and management of different aspects of Indian society. Government felt it necessary to review some of the institutions which had functioned during the British period to see what restructuring was required in the new context. There were several commissions on aspects of the educational system: the first Press Commission was set up in 1952 and there was a Film Enquiry Commission in 1951.

When Mrs Indira Gandhi joined the central government for the first time in 1964, she assumed responsibility for the Ministry of Information and Broadcasting, with cabinet rank. Broadcasting had been through a decade and more of rigid control while B.V. Keskar was at the helm of affairs as Minister of State, that is, without cabinet rank. Mrs Gandhi felt that broadcasting needed a breath of fresh air, and it was she who set up the first Enquiry Committee into All India Radio.

The Chanda Enquiry Committee Report 1966

This enquiry was headed by A.K. Chanda, a distinguished administrator and former Auditor-General of India. The Chanda Committee, as it is popularly known, made three major recommendations in its report which was published in 1966. It suggested that AIR be converted into a corporation run by a Board of Governors on the BBC model: that television be separated from radio and given a twenty-year development plan; and that the Vividh Bharati channel be commercialised and its profits ploughed back into radio for the improvement of programmes. After four years, the government rejected the first recommendation on the grounds that the time was not ripe for AIR to be converted into a corporation. While Government did not prepare a long-range plan for the development of TV, it did agree that the country needed TV and that it should be expanded within the available resources. Separation was effected only a decade later. During the Nehru era, government had taken the stand that India would do without TV because it was expensive. The Chanda Committee's proposal to commercialise the Vividh Bharati channel was accepted and brought into effect in 1967, though here also it took nearly ten years before the profits were actually made available to AIR.

The Verghese Working Group Report 1978

It was in this context that the Janata party proposed, as a major plank in its election manifesto, to give autonomy to AIR and Doordarshan. In August 1977, therefore, the government set up a Working Group under the chairmanship of George Verghese, a distinguished journalist, to work out proposals giving full autonomy to AIR and Doordarshan, consistent with accountability to Parliament. The Working Group was called upon to make recommendations on the form and structure of the autonomous organisation(s), finance, staffing and other allied matters. The Working Group submitted its Report in February 1978 in two volumes, the first containing the Group's sixty-five recommendations and the second the appendices of the extensive data collected during the course of the enquiry.

The Working Group recommended that AIR and Doordarshan should function under a single trust to be called Akash Bharati or the National Broadcast Trust. The autonomy of the Trust and its independence from government should be entrenched in the Constitution itself. The trust should consist of a chairman and trustees to be appointed by the President from a list of names proposed by the Chief Justice of India, the Chairman of the Union Public Service Commission and the Lok Pal (Ombudsman). (In effect a Lok Pal does not yet exist: legislation to create the position has yet to be passed by Parliament.) While a single Trust was envisaged for the whole country, the Working Group recommended a decentralised structure at the management level to facilitate quick decision-making and sensitivity to regional and local problems.

The Controller-General of Akash Bharati would be ex-officio Secretary of the Board of Trustees, and head of the Central Executive Board which would be responsible for the management of Akash Bharati. Thus a two-tier system was proposed with the Controller-General of Broadcasting providing an organic link between the two. The Chairman and three members of the Board of Trustees would be full-time workers. The Trust was required to report to Parliament through its budget and to present an annual report together with its accounts and the auditor's comments on them. The report said that while Members of Parliament have the inherent right to ask questions, it was hoped that they would refrain from doing so on day-to-day issues.

Among other things, the report gave the Trust the powers to licence educational institutions to run what were described as 'franchise stations'. Such stations would not be authorised to broadcast news or to accept commercial advertisements. It also recommended the setting up of a complaints board, a quasi-judicial body which would deal with complaints from the public provided the right of recourse to the Courts were waived.

After considering the report and suggestions made during the public debate which followed its publication, the government introduced a bill in Parliament to give autonomy to AIR and Doordarshan. The bill rejected the concept of trusteeship and the provision of constitutional safeguards for the proposed corporation. The two-tier system, decentralisation and franchise stations found no place in it. The broadcasting wing of the Ministry of Information and Broadcasting was not to be wound up; in fact, its Secretary and also the Secretary, Ministry of Finance, were to be ex-officio members of the Board of Governors of the proposed corporation. Financial control was to be maintained by the government and modifications in the procedure were proposed for the selection of the chairman of the corporation which suggested this would become a political appointment. Clause 23 of the Bill empowered government to issue directives to the corporation from time to time as it considered necessary. A copy of these directives was to be laid before each house of Parliament. The Bill had been referred to a joint select committee of the two Houses of Parliament and was to come up for discussion during the monsoon session of Parliament in July 1979. Because of the dissolution of the Lok Sabha (lower house), the bill lapsed.

The bill was thus a non-starter, but it nevertheless represents the farthest point to which the urge for autonomy has so far reached. It is, therefore, interesting to observe the reactions which the bill evoked.

The chairman and five members of the Working Group expressed their dissatisfaction with the bill in a joint press statement issued on 23 May 1979. They contended that the bill:

... offers something emasculated and confined with the executive continuing as the dominant influence... It leaves the Corporation dependent on the government for the composition of the single board proposed... Government directives may now be issued on any and every matter. That such directives shall subsequently be placed before Parliament is a delayed and inadequate safeguard since broadcasting is instant... Government as distinct from Parliament, budgetary control has been tightened in some degree.

The statement concludes as follows:

There seems something wrong with the rhetorical question: "What do you do when the Corporation misuses autonomy?" When the reason why the people want an independent Corporation is because the executive, abetted by a captive Parliament, shamelessly misused broadcasting during the Emergency, that is what has to be prevented for all time. Democracy is not something based on the pillar of only one institution, such as Parliament or the judiciary, however important it may be. It is a tapestry woven out of many institutions, of which a free, responsible and creative broadcasting system is one of the most significant.

On the other hand, L.K. Advani, then Minister for Information and Broadcasting, contended that the Working Group had in this respect exceeded its mandate. In a statement issued in Calcutta on 2 June 1979, he said the Committee had conceived of 'not just an autonomous Corporation but an independent constitutional status for AIR. The government is unable to accept this independent entity concept, but so far as the concept of autonomy is concerned it has gone far beyond the Chanda Committee's recommendations.' He argued that it was this latter concept which had been promised in the party's election manifesto.

Reactions in the press to the Prasar Bharati Bill appear to have been almost uniformly critical. Here are a few excerpts from editorials. The *Hindu* of Madras, in its editorial of 18 May, wrote that, 'Apart from creating a Corporation, which on paper seems to be the controlling authority, both All India Radio and Doordarshan will for all practical purposes be very much under the surveillance of the government.' Commenting on the objectives stated in the Bill that the corporation shall be *innovative, dynamic, flexible, democratic* and *responsive* to the people of India, the paper remarks, 'Quite unobjectionable, but a Corporation which continues to receive instruction from the government on matters of vital importance is hardly likely to be all that.'

The *Indian Express* stated on 18 May that, 'The principle of autonomy, to which the Janata Party and its government were pledged has all but been abandoned,' and the *Statesman* on May 23 that, 'Given the scope for official control and intervention indicated in the Bill, there is no prospect of a set-up which the government says will be innovative, dynamic, flexible, democratic and responsible to its opportunities and to the people of India.' The *Times of India,* 7 May, in its weekly Radio and TV column, held that when 'Shorn of all its verbiage, the Bill really confirms that the media will not only remain a monopoly, they will virtually remain a government monopoly.' *Hindustan Times,* 15 June, in a centre-page article claimed that 'The vast majority of Ministers made it known [when the Bill was presented in Parliament] in a casual manner that freedom had its dangers. Bureaucrats had the biggest say in the matter.' *Patriot,* 28 June, in a centre-page article asked, 'Haven't we been too much pre-occupied with the autonomy for broadcasting? The Bill does not underline any special concern for the social relevance of broadcasting and public discussions have slurred over it. Would the Select Committee now give it its due place and specify priorities?'

The Programme Staff Association of AIR and Doordarshan in a resolution adopted on 20 May said that the Bill had overlooked the true meaning of autonomy which involved 'restructuring of the two media to restore creative and functional freedom to the professionals and artists and removal of financial constraints and bureaucratic controls.'

One of the recommendations in the Verghese report which attracted a good deal of favourable comment pertains to the setting up of 'franchise stations'. It was envisaged that educational institutions should be granted a licence to operate a radio or television station.

These stations would not be empowered to broadcast news bulletins. The Group considered that franchise stations would 'bring variety and innovation to programmes', would provide 'an enormous stimulus to educational and extension programmes' and also open up avenues for 'a certain amount of programme access outside Akashvani and Doordarshan in the interest of diversity and competition'. A widely-voiced opinion was that franchise stations would, in a small way put an end to monopoly and the ills generally associated with it. Franchise stations found no place in the Prasar Bharati Bill and this was one of the major criticisms levelled against it.

Report of the Joshi Working Group on Software 1983

On 6 December 1982, Mrs Gandhi's government set up a Working Group to enquire into and report on the requirements of software for Doordarshan. The Group was asked to 'prepare a software Plan taking into consideration the main objectives of television of assisting in the process of social and economic development of the country and to act as an effective medium for providing information, education, and entertainment.' The Working Group was headed by Dr P.C. Joshi, Director of the Institute of Economic Growth, Delhi, and included thirteen members who were drawn from the fields of journalism, development and rural communication, education and science, the arts, and those concerned with women's and children's welfare. One member, a film maker, had considerable experience as a Producer in Doordarshan. The Additional Director-General of Doordarshan, an old AIR hand who had been trained in television at the BBC, was member-secretary. The Working Group was asked to report in four months but actually took a year. Government sat on the report for some eighteen months and it was placed on the table of the Lok Sabha, the Lower House of the Indian Parliament on 12 August 1985! Although it is now a public document and should be widely distributed, the Government has not done so. Copies of the report are still not available.

The report remains still-born and in the absence of opportunities for widespread study and debate cannot influence public opinion to any appreciable extent. It is, however, a valuable analysis of the programmes of Doordarshan and it is for this reason that it is dealt with at some length.

The report, which is unanimous, runs into three volumes: Volume 1 is the main report and recommendations; Volume 2 a summary of the recommendations and Volume 3 consists of appendices and the evidence recorded. The report is a sociological and economic study of India as it is today beset with problems of poverty and illiteracy, especially in the rural areas, inspired by a vision of its future as a socialist democracy with a definite personality of its own derived from its many-faceted culture. It is in this setting that the report defines the role which communication, especially television, can play in the modernising egalitarian process.

Technology, and here the reference is to satellite technology, can be used in at least two different ways. It can be used to build a Delhi-centric view of India, which also in effect means, 'promoting integration among the élites of different regions within the country on the basis of a common life-style characteristic of the new rich... and integrating the élites of the developing countries with the élites of the developed countries.' This use of technology has the effect of widening the gap between the rich and the poor within the country. On the other hand, Doordarshan can evolve a truly Indian personality if it acquires a sensitivity 'to socio-cultural requirements of the Indian situation at national, regional and local levels.' To this end the most urgent need is to decentralise the TV system and to give top priority to providing community sets in Indian villages for which adequate funds must be earmarked in the Seventh Plan (Chapter II, *paras 41-42*).

Annotating McLuhan and Brecht, the authors say, 'Software which does not evolve out of some form of participation is weak in authenticity and appeal... TV software is at its best when it presents uniqueness and diversity... at its worst when it offers uniformity and homogenization.' Doordarshan's future software should be 'a qualitatively new style'; 'the non-participatory, top-downwards [present] style is to be insensitive to its nature and possibilities,' (Ch. I, *para 50*).

While the Joshi Group was in the midst of its work, Mrs Indira Gandhi's government announced its special plan to set up relay transmitters to extend the TV system. The intention was, which has since been put into effect, to telecast from 8.30 PM to 10 PM daily a national programme which is relayed over the entire network. It is presented in Hindi and English and includes a news bulletin in each of these languages and other programmes including imported serials in English. This hardware plan cut at the roots of decentralising software. The report quoted one of its members as saying that 'The special Plan for TV expansion, to take the Delhi kendra's programmes of meretricious entertainment and government publicity to the middle and upper classes all over urban India, is the greatest communication aberration in the history of the Third World.' (Ch. III, *para 36.*)

In order to restore Doordarshan's original purpose of promoting social education and development the report recommends that each transmitter of the network be equipped with studios and facilities to produce programmes in the language or dialect of the local audience which are of relevance to them. This can be done in stages with make-shift studios and portable equipment to begin with. It rubs in the point that visuals are not self-sufficient, they need language to complete their meaning. (Ch. III, *para 81.*) And then the local community which is to be a participant in programme-making must view the programme. The central and state governments, nationalised banks and other agencies must come forward to provide at least one community-viewing set in each of India's 57,500 villages, though such sets have never to date touched the 10,000 mark. In this section, the report is critical of Doordarshan's conception of a national programme which is at best a regional programme radiated on the network.

Local participatory software, then, is the key to educational and developmental programming. This is entirely lacking in Doordarshan. The rural programmes suffer from being studio-based; they project the urban viewpoint on rural development. Family planning should be a major area of concern to Doordarshan but this implies that the government will have to resolve some basic issues if this programme can be projected as an integration of human needs, involving among other things the status of women. (Ch. VIII, *para 8.*) At least 50 per cent of Doordarshan's programme time should be given over to programmes which are socio-educational. Adequate funds should be provided and personnel should be posted at each kendra to discharge these functions.

The Group emphasises the importance of education through entertainment. It comes down heavily on the bulk of Doordarshan's entertainment programmes which are films or film-based. Most Indian films which find their way on to the TV screen are described as

an assault on aesthetic sensibility... which have a vulgarising and brutalizing effect on viewers... Even worse than the third-rate films screened in full are the compilations from such films, many of which are concentrated offerings of love duets accompanied by obscene gestures and scenes of imbecile hero chasing imbecile heroine round bushes or down a city street, teasing, harassing and finally winning her. (Ch. XI, *paras 2 & 3*.)

The report recommended the reduction of feature films by one per week at all centres. It noted that 'socially irrelevant foreign serials' were accounting for an increasing proportion of viewing time on the Doordarshan network. On behalf of the group, the Indian Institute of Mass Communication in Delhi carried out a quick survey to ascertain how many viewed the serials, how many comprehended them, and how many found them useful.

The results of the survey showed that foreign serials were viewed by 84.2 per cent of the respondents but only a small proportion of them had much familiarity with English. 22.4 per cent of the respondents did not even identify one of the serials as a detective serial! Many of the viewers could only recall funny incidents from the serials such as Lucy falling while trying to ski, or Father (in *Father, Dear Father*) getting something stuck on his nose! Viewing foreign serials, the report concludes, is largely without comprehension. Counting of heads may be relevant to the advertiser but is not of significance to the policy-maker concerned with effective communication. In May-July 1983, foreign serials accounted for 10.3 per cent of national programme time. It recommends that the telecast of 'foreign social comedy serials should be discontinued forthwith.' It suggests that Doordarshan turns away from 'its pathetic reliance on meretricious entertainment, local but commercial and debasing, or imported, to the rich cultural heritage of the country's folk and classical arts.' (Ch. XI, *paras 34 to 43*.)

In chapter XIV, paras 12 to 22, the Working Group has examined the sale of advertising in Doordarshan and referred with evident approval to the example of Indonesia which discontinued advertising on TV in 1979. While a minority were in favour of following Indonesia, the majority held that advertising is inseparable from a modern industrial economy and should continue. However it recommended that a fresh code for advertising on Doordarshan should be drawn up which would ensure that 'accepted national values' and good taste are not infringed. It noted that advertisements on Doordarshan tended to promote sexism and a few had been highly offensive. Doordarshan, it concludes, is not in the business of television for raking in maximum revenue; advertisements are incidental to its essentially educational role as a publicly-owned mass medium.

The report regrets that Doordarshan's newscasts and current affairs programmes are dominated by VIPs, their doings and statements, and of those of government. They 'show so little orientation towards the common people.' (Ch. V, *para 5*.) It quotes the second Press Commission for the view that although the newspapers are financed by big business they are much concerned with poverty and the problems of the common people. Dealing with the allegation of bias in news, the report says that Doordarshan plays down 'if not altogether blacks out negative news such as anti-government demonstrations... and incidents of violence'. (*Para 76*.) This may be due to self-censorship, which the report castigates as lack of professionalism. This same timidity and self-censorship dictates the subjects and choice of speakers in current affairs programmes. (*Para 81*.)

Dealing with allegations of governmental bias, it says that such complaints were made by the Congress (I) when the Janata were in power and opposition parties have made similar complaints against the Congress before and since. '... a firm line has yet to emerge between the ruling party and the government.' The Group have recommended the creation of an Ombudsman as a constitutional safeguard against misuse of the government-owned media on the lines of the Press Council. The Ombudsman would prevent or minimise bias in programmes and also protect Doordarshan's news personnel from unfair criticism. (*Para 126*.)

If there is to be an improvement, three conditions are necessary: (*i*) team-work between members of a professionally competent news crew; (*ii*) adequate resources of personnel, equipment, transport and operational flexibility in deploying them; and (*iii*) a higher quality of management which understands these and is committed to a policy appropriate to a large, democratic, developing country with a wide variety of languages and life patterns. (*Para 12*.) Towards this end, it recommends that the head of Doordarshan's news network should have the status of an Additional DG or DDG. He should be a person of high standing in the journalistic world and should be appointed on contract. Doordarshan should employ its own cadre of news personnel and stop the current practice of reserving senior news posts for officers of the Central Information Service

who may have no knowledge or experience of TV. At present, staff working in TV News and Current Affairs Units belong to two categories — senior posts such as those of controller, editor etc., are manned by officers of the CIS and are liable to transfer. Lower posts like those of producers, news cameramen, newsreaders are recruited exclusively for work in Doordarshan's news units. This bifurcation of staff impedes specialisation and team work. The report goes on to say, that the head of the TV news organisation should have powers to deploy his men for coverage at short notice. At present, even the Director-General cannot send a correspondent by air to cover an event because correspondents do not have the status to travel by air! To put an end to the Delhi-centricity of news the Group recommends a considerable extension of the number of correspondents and stringers employed throughout the country. It agrees, however, that 'Doordarshan's news wing is in a state of semi-starvation in terms of resources of all kinds, ranging from professional manpower, and equipment to working space and telephones.' (*Paras 81-94.*)

It was not among the terms of reference of the Working Group to make recommendations on the organisational structure of Doordarshan. But it felt compelled to do so because the hierarchical structure of the Information and Broadcasting Ministry, controlling the Director-General, leaves him little leeway to exercise initiative or leadership, and this is so all the way down the line. Since Mrs Gandhi's government had so recently turned down full autonomy for broadcasting, the Group does not raise the issue. It confines itself to defining 'functional autonomy' which the government has repeatedly declared itself in favour of giving. The Group suggests that the Ministry of Information and Broadcasting should be reorganised on the lines of the Railway Board and, like it, should be manned by officers who have grown up in TV and not by birds of passage drawn from the IAS. The Minister should be assisted by a body designated the National Doordarshan Council. The Minister would be the Chairman of the Council and the Director-General, convener. The Chief Engineer of Doordarshan would also be a member. Six or eight other members of the Council would be non-officials drawn from various fields such as education, science and technology, agriculture and rural development, communication research, advertising and sport. The Council would meet once a quarter, and its life would be three years.

The Council would discharge three functions: to review the performance of Doordarshan; to guard its professional and functional autonomy; to function as the Ombudsman in matters concerning news and current affairs. The Director-General of Doordarshan should be a person appointed on contract, with a proven record of excellence in social communication, as well as leadership qualities necessary for attracting creative talent in the service of the people.

The report expresses the view that had a body such as the Advisory Council been in existence in 1983, it would have been difficult to divert monies from the non-lapsable fund designed for software improvement, to set up relay transmitters for the expansion of the TV network. In this, I think they are certainly wrong. According to the procedure any change in the allotment of monies already accepted by the Planning Commission requires their approval. The Commission are extremely rigid in their attitude. Even reasonable changes as we have seen can be pursued only at a great risk and, mostly, departments do not dare to take the risk. However, the point to take note of is that the decision to divert 680 million rupees to the special plan for the expansion of TV was taken by the Prime Minister Mrs Gandhi and the Planning Commission was merely informed of what she had decided. (Ch. XXIV, *paras 25 to 32.*)

A most interesting and instructive part of the report consists of some half a dozen pages devoted to the reactions to programmes gathered in the course of the Group's meetings with people from different walks of life. Data of this kind is sadly lacking in India which is our justification for reproducing a handful of them. They figure in Chapter I.

We watch these films with our growing children along with our elders. And we feel ashamed. The children ask us what is going on. We have to tell lies. Adult films being shown to children, how do people in Delhi allow this? Have they no children about whose welfare they are concerned? Almost all outdoor activity and home work by children has been adversely affected by TV. What is the future of a country whose children are being turned into film addicts? (*Para 25.*)

Why these advertisements of expensive goods and gadgets, exploiting the female form for attracting attention? Why should Doordarshan promote consumerism? Is it not aggravating the dowry problem? There are atrocities on young girls who are not able to satisfy the growing appetite for those well-advertised goods and gadgets. (*Para 27.*)

See what they are offering us? This is done with our money but it is not for our welfare. Why do they not ask us? We can tell them what kind of programmes we want. We do not have the leisure to keep watching songs and dances. These are rich men's luxuries. Teach us skills, give us education, make us literate. Give us programmes on health, food, childcare. And about any schemes the government has for our benefit. (*Para 29.*)

Why should a programme for the village show only the village to us? Take us beyond the village. We also want to know about the world, about other countries or even about people in other parts of our big country; how they live and work, what is common and what is different among us. Can we never be like the town-folk? We are too poor to travel and see all the centres of pilgrimage in the four corners of India. Why do you not show us these holy places so that we have the satisfaction of having seen them? (*Para 30.*)

We want programmes in a language which we understand. But we also know that today's world is different from what it was in the past. One has to learn more than one language so that one can go to another place and can even work there. Why can't you teach our children more than one language? (*Para 32.*)

Why so much time to politics? To political leaders and state functions? Such over-publicity becomes irritating. Life has so many sides, why not touch other aspects of life? (*Para 37.*)

Why should Doordarshan be the mouth-piece of the government only? It should be the voice of all parts of the country and all sections of the people. (*Para 39.*)

Our part of India [Manipur State], has no caste system, no untouchability, no dowry deaths, no male domination of women. There are no idlers and parasites among us. Will your TV programmes introduce these bad things to our part also? Or will they tell the rest of the country to learn some of the good things from us? (*Para 40.*)

Why give only speeches on national integration? In many parts of the country people from different regions of India are learning to live together and taking over the food, dress, festivals, ceremonies, songs and dances of each other. This is national integration in actual life. Why cannot human-interest stories of emerging patterns of integrated living be presented? (*Para 43.*)

Doordarshan's programmes reproducing Bombay feature films violate every day in some way or the other the spirit of our Constitution. We want a secular, scientific, socialistic and democratic India. They have programmes which preach religiosity and superstition rather than scientific outlook, inequality between sexes and castes rather than equality, fatalism rather than activism, aversion to rather than dignity of manual labour, glorification of the élite classes rather than of the working people. Is not Doordarshan becoming the support of the backward-looking rather than of the forward-looking? This situation must be altered. (*Para 47.*)

Comment

The three enquiry reports are comprehensive documents which have made on an average two hundred and thirty recommendations each covering almost every aspect of broadcasting. They are spaced over a period of nearly twenty years and it is remarkable that they agree on several of their recommendations. Important among these are that AIR and Doordarshan recruit their own news personnel and be delinked from the Central Information Service, much more attention should be paid to non-formal education ensured through community listening and viewing if the electronic media are to fulfil their objective of bringing about social change.

Both the Chanda Committee and the Verghese Working Group pinned their faith on a corporation as an institution which would be able to function in an autonomous manner. Till the first half of the sixties there were some grounds for supposing that an autonomous institution could function in the Indian political and social milieu. But once the Congress Party's hold on the country broke down in 1967, it has become increasingly clear that none of the political parties would be prepared to release its hold on so powerful an instrument as broadcasting.

The concept of an autonomous corporation implies a liberal political system. As political parties become polarised, and inter-party strife takes on a new edge with violence and disruption intended to bring government to a standstill, autonomous institutions are pushed out of existence. This has been the trend in the last two decades, not only in India but also in Britain where the power and influence of the BBC have been drastically reduced through the introduction of ITV and the Independent Broadcasting Authority. Few believe today in the autonomy of the several hundred corporations which exist in India. Ministers can fire a Chairman of the Railway Board or a Director of Coal India Ltd. at will. Now the politicians appear to have joined battle with the judiciary and there is anxiety about the outcome. Would a corporation or a trust, in the Verghese Group's words, stand any chance of success?

True, the Group tried to provide safeguards in the constitution itself. While the Chanda Committee said it would leave the nomination of the chairman and members of the Board of Governors to the good sense of the government (*Para 699*), the Working Group recommended that they should be appointed by the President from a panel proposed by the Chief Justice of India, the Chairman of the .Public Service Commission and the Lok Pal or Ombudsman (*Para 6.24*). The Verghese Group seemed to be unrealistic in some of their recommendations, and to name the Lok Pal as one of the nominators is one example. Ten years have passed and legislation for the creation of the office of the Lok Pal has not come into existence! To hope that a corporation could function autonomously in the Indian situation was a slender hope indeed, but the public, like those who have worked in broadcasting, were clutching at straws.

The separation of television from radio was recommended by the Chanda Committee but negated by the Verghese Working Group. The Chanda Committee was of the view that television differs from radio 'in important matters of technique, financing of operations and planning and execution of programmes.' (*Para 776*). It considered that AIR was not 'organizationally and financially equipped to shoulder this responsibility' namely that of organising and developing Doordarshan (*para 778*). The Working Group while recognising that the skills and techniques of the two media are not entirely the same, said that 'total separation would add greatly to costs and create its own problems.' Moreover,

any national communications policy ... of which broadcasting would obviously constitute an important part, must call for a multi-media approach... the two services are complementary and therefore require unified and coordinated direction... In all cases other than the actual production of programmes such as administration, personnel, accounts, reference and research, audience, housing, transport and welfare, and even news, there would have to be common services. (*Paras 421-423.*)

In the late sixties, the Commonwealth Broadcasting Association had organised a seminar to discuss the pros and cons of introducing television as an organisation separate from the existing radio set-up. The experience of various countries facing this problem was pooled and some pertinent issues were identified and analysed. This data was available in AIR and the Ministry. But the question was never seriously examined. It seemed to be assumed, especially by those who had some experience of working in Doordarshan and by the Ministry, that television must be separate. The Working Group's arguments seem to me to be valid. Specialisation at production and technical levels must be provided and this can be as well done under one umbrella as it can be accomplished under two. The crucial point it seemed to me was that if radio and television remained a single organisation, whether as a Corporation or under government control, it would be in a far better position to resist gratuitous interference from the Ministry and other pressure groups. A small and new organisation such as Doordarshan, without firmly established procedures would easily succumb. And this is what has happened in the last ten years. It is generally acknowledged today, even by those in different departments of government who are themselves responsible for bullying Doordarshan into doing wrong things, that AIR is by far the more efficient of the two. I will not deny that AIR was not 'organizationally and financially equipped to launch television,' as stated by the Chanda Committee. But who else was then to do it? In 1975, SITE and three new Doordarshan kendras got going within a period of four months. AIR's resources were stretched to the limit, and much of the cream of programme and technical staff was drawn off to make the expansion of Doordarshan possible. It is true that habits, including those acquired in thinking in terms of radio, die hard; they can be and have been carried into television, like the pervasive vulgarity of the Indian film. But it is naive to suppose that Doordarshan staff are incapable of seeing the difference between radio and television. If television functions basically as radio with a picture added it is because of constraints on the staff and the authority's fear of what the camera can reveal.

The Joshi Working Group's report marks a decided advance on its predecessors in respect of those areas of programming encompassed by the concepts of distance learning or non-formal education. The earlier reports had stressed the need for providing community listening and viewing, for coordination of rural programming with extension services and so on. The Joshi Report goes to the heart of the matter. It says, 'The communication activity can only complement and supplement the real activity that physically brings about change in the field and in the lives of the people. If the reality falls short, communication efforts — no matter how masterly in technique and presentation — will at best remain ineffective and at worst will backfire.' Referring to the government's objectives of universal health, education and reduction of the poverty line to 10 per cent, the report continues, 'We believe that these separate programmes will have to be interwoven into a viable package for action and communication efforts similarly dovetailed to address human needs, if headway is to be made...' (Chapter IX *paras 5 & 6*). Without political, economic and social action by the Government, communication cosmetics will get us nowhere.

A small point which troubled me about the Verghese Working Group Report was their proposal to change the name of Akashvani to Akash Bharati. In English, in place of All India Radio (AIR), they proposed National Broadcasting Trust (NBT). There is a craze in modern India to change the names of roads, hospitals, medical colleges and so on. How easy it is! Sometimes it is merely confusing, as when you want to get your bearings in a city and find that road names have changed. Sometimes the results can be more serious. Institutions have a history and a reputation (for good or for ill) and they are known by their names to thousands, well beyond the national boundaries. No worthwhile purpose is served by wiping out their identity. The new name proposed by the Working Group was a howler. The initials NBT stand for the National Book Trust which has been in existence since 1957.

The Future of the Broadcasting System

6

Government Control Versus Autonomy

At a press conference on 7 July 1985, Mr Rajiv Gandhi said that AIR and Doordarshan are not yet ripe for autonomy. On 15 March 1948, his grandfather Jawaharlal Nehru addressing the Constituent Assembly where the Constitution was framed, said 'My own view of the set-up for broadcasting is that we should approximate as far as possible to the British model, the BBC; that is to say, it would be better if we had a semi-autonomous corporation. Now I think that is not immediately feasible.'

What both of them assumed, and what most Indians have accepted in the thirty-seven years intervening between these statements is that it is for the executive or the government to decide in what manner and to what extent governmental control would be lifted. Whatever form it takes it is a 'gift' from government. And so hopes ran high when Mrs Gandhi set up the Chanda Committee, and over thirteen years later, in 1977, when the Janata Government set up the Verghese Working Group. In the end, there was bitter disappointment in both cases.

What no one questioned until recently, is the right of the government to control broadcasting. No one raised the point that Article 19, 1(a) which guarantees freedom of thought and expression and which is the bedrock of the freedom of the press, equally guarantees freedom of broadcasting. It was taken for granted that while the press is free, broadcasting is a central subject and this means control by the Central Government. It is true that the Verghese Working Group in Para 5.20 of their report distinguishes between the Government's right to licence transmitters (which it concedes) and the act of broadcasting, viz, programming. The Working Group failed to note that the government has no inherent right to be the sole organiser and presenter of programmes. In fact, Article 19, 1(a) would seem to preclude it from doing so. On the analogy of the press, broadcasting programmes should be in the hands of diverse groups to ensure access to different shades of opinion. There has not been a situation in which there was only one newspaper in India. However, during the Emergency, four news agencies were incorporated into a single news-gathering organisation under central government control. When the Emergency was lifted, and normal democratic functioning was restored, the news agencies became separate again. The argument was that there must be free access to sources of news and this could be ensured only if there are several such sources.

If the freedom of the press is based on this Article and requires no further endorsement through an amendment of the Constitution, as has been argued by the second Press Commission, it can be charged that nothing further is necessary in the case of broadcasting either. To have access to all shades of opinion through the medium of broadcasting is the right of every individual in India, and is provided for under that very article of the Constitution which guarantees freedom of thought and expression, and ensures a free press. No doubt a newspaper has to be licensed, but the government cannot arbitrarily refuse a licence nor can it stop a newspaper from functioning provided it does not offend against certain decencies, under Clause 2 of Article 19 which we referred to in our discussion of the AIR Code. If an individual or a group of persons, basing themselves on this Article, have the right to set up a newspaper, and if as a result there are hundreds of newspapers in the country, how can government persist in maintaining a monopoly over broadcasting? It is true of course that the number of frequencies available for transmission is limited, and they must be regarded as a scarce national resource. Broadcast frequencies therefore cannot be assigned to any person or group without careful planning. From this, it simply does not follow that government has any right of monopoly over them. On the other hand, it can be argued that in insisting on maintaining a monopoly the government is violating a fundamental right guaranteed under the Constitution. So indeed argued Justice P.A. Chaudhuri at a seminar in 1984, and others, including Minoo Masani, have agreed that the government's monopoly should be challenged in the Supreme Court. Media autonomy is not a gift which the government gives to the people; it is a right which must be wrested from the executive through the courts.

A.G. Noorani, a distinguished lawyer and a member of the

Verghese Working Group has made a separate point in two articles in the *Indian Express*, and also in *Seminar* No. 292 (December 1983). His contention is that even if broadcasting is run by government, it has an obligation under Article 14 of the Constitution which guarantees equality before the law, and Article 19, 1(*a*) relating to freedom of thought and expression, to function in a fair and impartial manner. He quotes a Supreme Court ruling as follows: 'Whatever be its activity the government is still the government and is subject to restraints inherent in its position in a democratic society. The constitutional power conferred on the government cannot be exercized by it arbitrarily or capriciously or in an unprincipled manner. It has to be for the public good....' The conclusion that Mr Noorani draws is that 'the law is not in doubt and its arm can certainly reach well inside the news rooms.' What is needed is documentation and proof by the opposition parties or by any public body for that matter, that AIR and Doordarshan have been unfair and arbitrary in their presentation of opinion on public issues.

The Verghese Working Group did not accept either of these points, although its chapters on autonomy are penetrating and inspiring. In rejecting the idea of setting up a corporation under an Act of Parliament in para 5.8 it said that such a Corporation could be dissolved by a new Act. Further in Para 5.9 it recommended that 'the autonomy of the corporation and its independence from government control should be entrenched in the Constitution itself...' And these statements show that, in the Working Group's view, Article 19, 1(*a*) by itself does not guarantee the freedom of broadcasting, and to ensure this at least 'the fundamental principles of the national broadcasting Corporation should be written clearly into the Constitution'. (Para 5.10). The point that government itself cannot run AIR and Doordarshan in an arbitrary fashion and that Government can be compelled by the courts to act on principles of fairness is simply not raised.

Yet another proposal has been made recently by the Chief Minister of Karnataka, Rama Krishna Hegde, who belongs to the Janata party. He circulated among members of parliament and others a paper in which he urged that State Governments, who so desire, and are prepared to bear the costs, should be provided a channel on TV for educational purposes, especially for rural areas. He argues that the present central monopoly of broadcasting is against the spirit of a federal union. He draws attention to the clauses of the Government of India Act 1935, which we have quoted in chapter 2 to show that even the British government conceded that the provinces and the princely states had the right to set up their own broadcasting stations which should not be necessarily interfered with. Mr Hegde has also reproduced a Note prepared by Dr Pattabhi Sitaramayya, a former Congress President and a member of the Constituent Assembly. This Note, which was placed before India's constitution-making body, advocated 'concurrent jurisdiction over broadcasting.' Mr Hegde points out that INSAT IC (now scheduled for operation in 1987) will have two transponders and will provide four separate TV channels. 'These can surely be made available initially to four of the states which are keen on operating separate channels.' This arrangement, he emphasises, in no way challenges the Constitution and its current interpretation. (Mr Hegde's paper, to which Dr Sitaramayya's Note is attached as an appendix is available in *Seminar*, No. 319, March 1986).

Mr Hegde's suggestion may be welcome so far as it would loosen the central monopoly over broadcasting and would be appreciated especially by the non-Congress ruled states. However, this arrangement, if accepted, would still mean that the party in power in the states would be in a position to publicise its viewpoint. It would not automatically mean a more democratic use of the broadcast media. If we go by recent experience, the non-Congress governments do not have a savoury reputation. Corruption has been as rampant among them as elsewhere. They have each one of them been guilty of trying to trample on civil liberties, and in the case of Andhra Pradesh in particular to suppress the press. A second channel, controlled by the states, may be a boon to some political parties but it would compound the propaganda, dullness and narrow-mindedness already displayed on the existing central government controlled channel. I cannot, therefore, support this move.

A few private bodies have made demands for setting up radio stations. The authorities in charge of the Tirupati temple have been raising this issue from time to time over the last fifteen years. The Akali Dal made a similar demand for setting up a radio station in the Golden Temple in the late seventies. At the beginning of the same decade the municipal authorities in Bangalore wanted to establish a wire broadcasting service. Only one case was taken to the High Court, in Delhi. This happened when the government turned down a request by P.L. Lakhanpal, editor of the *Radio Times* in the late sixties. The case came up before a Division Bench of the Delhi High Court in 1982. Mr Lakhanpal's case was dismissed. (See AIR 1982, Delhi 167). From a perusal of the judgement it would appear that the rejection was based chiefly on the following considerations: first, that if everybody were to be given permission to run a radio station there would be chaos since frequencies were limited and people would be impinging on each other's channels. Although the right to freedom of expression on radio can be claimed, it does not follow that each person has a right to own a radio station. Second, the judgement said that the petitioner had applied to operate a 100-watt station, which would have very little coverage and a radio station of this kind would not meet any long-felt need of the public. In short, the petitioner had not made a good case why he should be given a licence to run a broadcasting station. The judgement appears thus to leave the door open for a change in the government's policy if a formula were evolved which would avoid chaos on the spectrum and would be in accordance with natural justice.

Justice P.A. Chaudhuri and A.G. Noorani have rendered a signal service by drawing attention to the legal redress which is available to listeners and viewers of AIR and Doordarshan. However, their views need to be disseminated among a wider public and action needs to be taken to test their validity in the Supreme Court. Moreover unless the political parties jointly and severally, take a stand on removing government control nothing can be expected.

Let us suppose that a case were taken to the Supreme Court, and that the Court asked the government to ensure fair coverage or ruled that the governmental monopoly is ultra vires of the Constitution. A major constitutional victory would be won. But would it be enough to ensure the proper day-to-day implementation of fairness?

The answer is clear: No. What is most needed is an intelligent, alert staff capable of taking an independent and objective view of events. What has been happening over the years is a severe erosion in the quality of the news and programme staff working in AIR and Doordarshan. A person of poor mental calibre is incapable of forming an independent judgement. He will be cautious, play for safety, because he will fear that if questioned he will not be able to defend himself. The lack of enterprise, the dullness and partisanship of programmes stem largely from this cause, the poor calibre of programme and news staff. How has this come about and what must now be done to obtain for AIR and Doordarshan the type of adventurous, imaginative and sensitive personnel which radio and TV deserve?

In the early years AIR recruited its own news staff. Some distinguished people served it, such as Nirad C. Chaudhuri, Prem Bhatia, till recently Editor of the *Tribune*, Pran Chopra, former Editor of the *Statesman*, and G.L. Obhrai who headed the Media Division of UN, to mention just a few. These men understood the demands of the spoken word, the concentration necessary in a ten-minute bulletin and the immediacy of a news despatch which could bring a situation vividly before the listener's mind. The formation of the Central Information Service finished all that. AIR and Doordarshan got instead a stream of colourless individuals incapable of writing or voicing a despatch or using the camera to get a telling picture. One quality however they developed and carried with them always — the capacity of drum-beating for the Government (there are notable exceptions of course, persons who because of their earlier association with the press or long periods of posting in AIR news, appreciate the responsibilities of a news organisation). One cannot blame them, for that is what they are hired to do in all departments of the Ministry of Information and Broadcasting, with the exception of the news and current affairs programming of AIR and Doordarshan. The Chanda Committee, the Verghese Working Group and now the Joshi Working Group have recommended that the news rooms should be manned by staff employed by these services. The news staff of AIR and Doordarshan should be provided with opportunities for promotion as heads of stations, Deputy Directors-General and be in the running for the post of Director-General. (There have been precedents: the current Director-General of Radio Pakistan comes from their news division and I, myself, served my apprenticeship in AIR's news room.)

In the early days of AIR, Fielden and Bokhari were in touch with the heads of prestigious colleges and Vice-Chancellors to collect from them the names of promising young persons completing their education who were looking out for jobs. Such people were inducted into broadcasting. Mainly, they were those who might otherwise have been interested in a career in education. A programme assistant in AIR drew a salary at least 50 per cent higher than a college lecturer. In a new and rapidly expanding department promotions came quickly and it was not surprising to come across Station Directors in their early thirties. However, while scales elsewhere improved, those in broadcasting slumped. Since independence the remuneration offered to college and university teachers has improved vastly and is responsible for the fact that, in our best institutions, the quality of education can be favourably compared with what can be found anywhere in the world. But what obtains for university teachers still does not compare with the heaven-born Indian Administrative Service, the Foreign Service, or even with the Class I services in the Government of India. University teachers even in Delhi have been on strike twice since 1983 demanding better prospects which would reduce stagnation, provide more housing and the like.

Where do the programme staff of AIR and Doordarshan figure in the governmental set-up? Programme Executives, at the bottom rung of the ladder are Class II Gazetted Officers. The scale is low and there is a ceiling where one may stagnate for years before one is promoted or selected to the next higher post of ASD. The same may happen at the next two stages above, at the posts of SD (ordinary grade) and SD (selection grade). Above that are just about a dozen posts in the two departments taken together, of DDG and Additional DG who rank as Directors and Joint Secretaries in the Government. At the apex are the two DGs with the pay and status of Additional Secretaries and at least one of them has to be an IAS officer. At the moment, both the DGs are from the IAS.

As if the scales themselves were not pitiful enough, the promotion prospects make things far worse. There was a time some twenty years ago, when programme staff would retire without a single promotion in their service career. For this the responsibility must be borne by Dr Keskar, who introduced the Producer cadre of writers and artists who were appointed entirely according to his personal fancies. It took two decades to bring some system and order into the mess he had created. During this period of nearly twenty years there were hardly any appointments to the cadre of Programme Executives. It is a wonder that AIR continued to function; it is a tribute to the dedication of the staff who remained loyal to the department.

Things are somewhat better today, but not much. Persons who have served fifteen years or more remain on the bottom rung of the ladder. It would be unusual to find a Station Director this side of forty.

Small wonder then that when AIR advertises posts for Programme Staff through the UPSC, the response is poor. Having served or several selection boards, I can say that few of those who apply come up to the required standard — AIR and Doordarshan are dustbins for those who have nowhere else to go. On the other hand Yuv Vani has attracted talent of the first order. People such as Ramu Damodaran, Rajiv Mehrotra, Divya Raina and Sunit Tandon, to name only a few, who did programmes in their student days, exhibited the type of mental qualities which could make for first rate programmers — they were imaginative, critical, alert and sensitively articulate. But when it came to choosing a career they had to turn elsewhere; AIR and Doordarshan simply could not provide them the wherewithal and the opportunities in which they could flower.

Predictably, the Third Pay Commission which reported to government in July 1986 did not have the imagination to see that a revolution in the pay-scales and prospects of broadcasters is necessary to pull it out of the present mess. August bodies such as Pay Commissions are rooted in the status quo. The Commission started with the fact that the post of PEX is a Class II post. Everything else followed from that. There has been a little patchwork here and there. We are informed that an Indian Broadcasting Service for Programme Staff is in the offing and it might be notified within six months. There will only be cadre formulation of what already exists! Senior officials seem to think that this was revolutionary; as they say in Hindi, a mountain gave birth to a mouse.

The legal issue for the freedom of broadcasting is just one of its preconditions. If this freedom is not to exist on paper only, we need an overhaul of the programme and news staff, and the replacement of feeble-minded nonentities by adventurous and alert persons always ready to test the frontiers of what is permissible. The prospect of attracting such persons within the government set-up is as we have seen remote. Private broadcasting organisations would be very open in comparison. So in the long run, a plurality of broadcasting organisations seems the more practical of the two alternatives.

A sound legal framework, a staff committed to the freedom of broadcasting — these are two basic requirements. There is a third: a self-denying ordinance of interference from those at the helm of affairs, be they a management board of a private company, trustees of a corporation or ministers. Interference has gone on for the last thirty-seven years in broadcasting. Dr Keskar was prophetic when he declared, 'There has been interference, and there shall be more and more interference.'

While there was a qualitative difference between the Janata government and the one it replaced, interference in appointments and in programmes continued in matters which cannot be dismissed as trivial. This culture of interference from the top must be changed and the change does not occur when we start referring to an organisation as a corporation instead of a government department. Autonomy and credibility have to be fought for every day; the struggle is not won or lost with one battle.

The government's alternative to autonomy, about which there has been much talk in the last five years, is 'functional autonomy' for AIR and Doordarshan. In November 1980 the government set up a high-powered Advisory Committee of fourteen members under the chairmanship of G. Parthasarathy. Mr Parthasarathy served Mrs Gandhi in several important and delicate assignments. He has been, and still is, chairman of the Policy Planning Committee of the Ministry of External Affairs, was India's representative on the Executive Board of UNESCO and the first Vice-Chancellor of Jawaharlal Nehru University in Delhi. On the broadcasting side, the Committee includes such personalities as V.K. Narayana Menon, formerly DG, AIR, and P.V. Krishnamoorthy, Doordarshan's first DG, when it became a separate department.

The Parthasarathy Committee is thus a Standing Committee and it is not required to release for public consumption its various recommendations to government for the improvement of the media. One of the major issues it was expected to examine and define is that of 'functional autonomy' in its various aspects. However, in five years the Committee has achieved nothing and appears to be more or less defunct.

Where is autonomy most needed?

Autonomy and Programmes

Where programme output is concerned the areas which are most in need of 'functional autonomy' are news and current affairs and programme support for development. The framework for news coverage and current affairs is clear enough and those in charge should be left alone to deal with issues on merit. There is no doubt that there has been direct interference by the Ministry in news coverage and more so in Doordarshan than in AIR. Since the Congress (I) came to power in January 1980 the Director of the News Services

Division was changed three times in the course of two years, allegedly on political grounds. Several producers in Doordarshan were also transferred on similar grounds. Recorded versions of several party speeches of Mrs Gandhi and of Mr Rajiv Gandhi have frequently been broadcast over AIR and Doordarshan, contrary to established convention.

The Joshi Working Group's recommendation for the appointment of an Ombudsman to monitor the output of Doordarshan's news department and to protect its personnel from harassment by the government is welcome and should be tried out. His ambit should be widened to take in AIR.

A tendency which has been growing in recent years is to dictate to the media what shall be done and how often to support the government's development programmes. This trend reached its climax during the twenty months of the Emergency when AIR and Doordarshan had to supply to the Ministry statistics for each station or centre of the number of programmes broadcast on each point of the government's twenty-point programme. The Janata Government required more or less similar data on publicity for prohibition. This tendency has to be checked not only in the name of functional autonomy but indeed if media support for development is to yield positive results.

Autonomy and Administration

In recent years some progress has been made by the government of India in delegating financial and administrative authority to heads of departments. Heads of Departments, among them the Directors-General of AIR and Doordarshan, now exercise almost all powers enjoyed by Ministers under the administrative and financial rules. These concern matters which are common to all departments of government such as appointment of staff, payment of travelling and per diem allowances, disciplinary procedures, purchase of equipment and stores, and the like.

The general delegation of powers on such matters is undoubtedly of importance and is certainly helpful to the Directors-General in running their departments, but they do not cover the special requirements of broadcasting and television, on which the Ministry has been reluctant to loosen its grip. The category of staff in AIR and Doordarshan known as Staff Artists are peculiar to broadcasting and the terms and conditions of service of Staff Artists are unique in the Government of India. But it remains the Ministry of Information and Broadcasting which decides on most matters of importance concerning the remuneration, conditions of service and appointment of Staff Artists. Even overtime payments to them at stations have to be approved by the Ministry. Many categories of Staff Artists in AIR have been stagnating for years because of limited opportunities for promotion; but the Directors-General can do little to ameliorate their condition. Equally, the Directors-General cannot alter the scales of payment to musicians, actors, writers and other performers.

The Directors-General find themselves hamstrung because of standardised rules and procedures which operate uniformly in all departments of government. Little attention is paid to the peculiar needs of an organisation in terms of the functions it is required to perform. For example on the question of providing telephones to staff the criterion is status, especially for one at the residence. If a news correspondent is not of the status of an Under Secretary it is next to impossible to give him a telephone at his residence. Again, economy in the use of transport will be applied uniformly to all departments of government, including AIR and Doordarshan. Obviously there can be little functional autonomy for the media if they have to work in accordance with procedures appropriate to a secretariat.

The Case for Commercial Broadcasting

A word or two more (apart from the exposé provided by the Joshi Working Group) is necessary in the case for commercial broadcasting, which foreign observers complain has gone almost by default. Foreigners frequently contrast the highly developed Indian cinema with the poor showing of AIR and Doordarshan. If cinema has been able to achieve its present pre-eminence as a result of private enterprise, why should radio and TV not be permitted to flower in the same way?

There is today, and has been since Independence, a lobby for commercial broadcasting sponsored by merchants' associations, advertisers and the like. This lobby however did not cut much ice with the Chanda Committee and Verghese Working Group, as evidenced in their Reports. It has found little support in the press or in other fora influential in formulating public opinion despite the fact that Doordarshan has gone commercial with a vengeance in the last two years.

The reasons for public indifference to commercial broadcasting are not far to seek. The purely political argument, whatever its merit, has already been stated. The international community, no doubt, forms its opinion of the Indian cinema industry as a result of viewing the many prize-winning films screened at festivals abroad. These films are not at all representative of the output of the industry; they have been produced in spite of it. The picture at home is very different. The general run of Indian films has been described by our critics as politically and socially reactionary. Control over what can be exhibited, and therefore over production, lies with the film distributors and their sole interest is the box office. Production costs have rocketed sky-high, out of which film stars have made their packets. By and large the film world has a bad name for corruption, widespread use of black money, and vulgarity. For the intelligentsia the example of the film industry is an argument against the commercialisation of broadcasting.

There is also another important factor. Apart from providing entertainment and news, broadcasting is expected to serve national objectives some of which may not be commercially paying. Government's policy has been that where a national service is involved, it cannot be left to the private sector. For instance, when the domestic air services were nationalised in the fifties the argument was that private carriers were not interested in the unpopular routes. On the other hand, remote areas (to which there is little traffic) are important from the point of view of national service precisely because of their isolation. And exactly this would apply in the case of broadcasting. Why should private finance, represented by the advertiser, be interested in remote areas, which lack industry and purchasing power? What markets can they offer to the seller of goods?

These theoretical considerations have been shown to be valid since Doordarshan went in for sponsored programmes in a big way from 1983. The sponsors have understandably not been interested in programmes for the eradication of illiteracy, for primary education in the villages or for sanitation and health. No sponsor has come forward to fund any programmes of this nature in the last two years. The Joshi Working Group's Report is a scathing indictment of Doordarshan's sell-out to consumerism but the situation has worsened since the Group submitted its report and soap opera serials came into their own. Iqbal Masud's comment at the conclusion of *Hum Log* (We People) which had a record run of 256 episodes and on *Khandaan* (which deals with family problems in the changing social setting and stars the famous writer-producer-actor Girish Karnad), was 'They propagate love for authority, order and tradition. Tears, laughter, pregnancies, death — everything is played up and trivialized.'

The Future of Radio

A National Radio Channel

As has been pointed out, the percentage of national or network programmes put out by the radio service in Hindi and English is about 5 per cent. The vast majority of programmes are in the regional languages. Thus, for persons who for business or other reasons live and work outside their linguistic region, there is little to get from their local station. As a result linguistic minorities in each state have been making demands for programmes in their respective languages. These demands have been conceded and in several cases many stations broadcast in four or more languages. With single-channel stations, especially, this arrangement of splitting up transmission time does not satisfy any one. On the other hand the relay of national programmes at peak listening times, while of interest to linguistic minorities, is irritating for those confined to the regional language. There is also the larger consideration of fostering national unity which has to be taken into account. If the centrifugal forces of lingualism are to be countered some measures must be taken to encourage listening to programmes presented in a national perspective through the national language and English. It was in this context that AIR had proposed in the Fifth Plan a National Channel carried on one or more super-power transmitters which would be available in all parts of the country for some eighteen hours in the day. This project did not get off the ground during the Fifth Plan, and little progress has been made in the Sixth Plan. Many in the organisation believe that the National Channel could play an important role in creating a national consciousness. It would also serve a real need. It is well-known that English language broadcasts by foreign radio stations command considerable listening in several parts of the country. There is of course an intrinsic interest in listening to what other stations have to offer! But one reason is that AIR itself has little by way of news, comment and entertainment for Indians in far-flung areas of the country who do not know the regional language.

The National Channel as so far conceived would function on a somewhat similar basis to the External Services. The studios would be located in Delhi with co-axial linkage with the super-power transmitter in Nagpur. Nagpur has been chosen for the location because it is nearly in the centre of India. After this transmitter comes into operation other supporting transmitters are proposed to be added to improve the area of coverage. News bulletins, commentaries, newsreels and the like would be contributed by NSD. The organisation responsible for the National Channel would have its staff and resources for the production of programmes and would additionally draw on the stations for material. Translation of scripts written originally in the regional languages would be translated into Hindi and English. AIR has considerable experience in preparing programmes of this kind for the General Overseas Service in English and for the Urdu Service which function under the Director of External Services.

Local Radio

There seems to be considerable faith inside the organisation, in government, and among the public generally, in radio's efficiency as an instrument of education and as an agent in social change. The part which radio has played in educating farmers is frequently cited. It is held that 'local radio' where there will be considerable participation of the community in discussing local affairs will act as an important catalyst in improving the quality of life. The ITU allocation provides AIR with 352 low-power transmitters of up to 1Kw each which will share three reserved frequencies. AIR's long-range objective is to provide each district headquarters, and there are approximately 350 districts in the country, with its own local radio station for this purpose. As we have seen only one such station has been set up so far. Five more are projected in the Seventh Plan.

Radio for the Masses

As we have seen, the total number of radio sets in the country is woefully inadequate and only 25 per cent of these are in the rural areas. The basic problem is poverty. Not until we solve that problem can the question of radiu becoming a mass medium arise. However, even in the present context the following suggestions which have emerged at State Information Ministers' Conferences, for promoting the sale of radio sets in the rural areas, deserve to be considered:

(a) Establishing retail outlets or dealerships for sale of radio sets. Setting up of shops sponsored by state governments could be helpful.

(b) Maintenance and repair facilities should be provided at Block Development Offices in the rural areas. At present repair facilities are not available and in remote areas even torch cells are not to be found in the market except at district headquarters.

It will thus be seen that although much lip service is paid to the reach of the radio as a means of communication with the masses, especially those who are illiterate and in remote areas, little concrete has been done to make it easier for these people to acquire and maintain radio receivers.

The Future of Television

In his report, Dr Joshi has pinpointed the priorities for the development of Doordaishan if it is to redeem itself and get down to serving the people as a catalyst for development. Doordarshan kendras must start producing programmes in their regional languages and deal with the problems of the audiences to whom they are directed. Indeed we are informed that full-fledged kendras with their own studios in all the 'major' state capitals are the first priority in the Seventh Plan. Twelve such centres are to be set up in the next five years. The programmes radiated by each centre, made available throughout the state through micro-wave links or by satellite, is described as the primary service of Doordarshan. The national service is already there and will of course continue. A third tier to the service will be the local service. This will be presented by means of a second channel at centres such as Calcutta and Madras. At twelve centres some sort of studio and programme production facilities will be provided for a local channel.

The Seventh Plan gives high priority to the north-eastern region. Studio facilities are to be improved at Guwahati, and some sort of production facilities, if not regular studios, are to be provided in the capitals of tribal states such as Kohima, Imphal, Shillong, Aizawl and Itanagar.

The Ministry's record on the construction of studios has not been encouraging. The Calcutta and Lucknow TV centres were commissioned in 1975 and were housed in makeshift studios. Calcutta for instance, had no control room and had to use the control panel of an OB van which was parked alongside the studio building!

Eleven years elapsed before the Calcutta kendra got its permanent studios and Lucknow is still in its temporary buildings! The drive for making arrangements for software is not a fraction of that which goes into the setting up of transmitters. The DG Doordarshan told a seminar in Delhi at the beginning of January 1986 that when all Seventh Plan Schemes were implemented the country would have 192 TV transmitters and fourteen studios.

Studio facilities in state capitals to produce programmes in a single regional language will not take us very far, considering the linguistic variations in the country. An obvious example is Kashmir where transmitters already exist at Jammu, where the language is Dogri, and Kargil and Leh, where the people need to be addressed in Ladakhi. And what about a language policy in the tribal states of the northeast? I wonder what thinking has gone into this question. They have to avoid the mistake of AIR, of proliferation of dialects and find one or two languages which can make for real communication. A proper mix of regional and sub-regional languages will have to be worked out.

On the nature of the software which Doordarshan should be producing, Dr Joshi has given the guidelines. The distinction between education and entertainment is not dichotomous. One does not necessarily exclude the other. However, Doordarshan needs to address itself to the problems of removing illiteracy, about which nothing has been done so far. In-school educational programmes have not been improved nor have viewing facilities been extended during the last decade. In fact the number of sets in schools in Delhi and Bombay has gone down during the last four years. It was over 800 in 1981 and is just over 500 today. In non-formal education the lessons of SITE must be taken seriously if real gains are to be made. We must see through the facade of the so-called UGC programmes on higher education which are a waste of satellite time and money.

What finds no priority in the Seventh Plan, is the provision of community viewing sets in the villages and there are nearly six hundred thousand of them. As before, the centre wants to throw the responsibility on the states and the states argue that they have no resources and want to pass the buck back to the centre. Since the centre has not involved the states in the development of Doordarshan and they have no say in its programme output, the states can have no stake in it and one cannot blame them for being hostile to a medium used for pumping out Congress party propaganda. This is a major issue between the centre and the states and it cannot be resolved solely on the financial issue of the states providing the sets and looking after their maintenance. If they contribute, they must get a return in the shape of a positive share in determining what goes on the screen.

A National Communications Policy

India does not have an explicitly defined national communications policy. There is a well-known science policy resolution adopted by Parliament in 1958 associated with the late Prime Minister Jawaharlal Nehru. Among its objectives is to secure for the people the benefits which accrue from the acquisition and application of scientific knowledge. This is to be achieved, by fostering and sustaining scientific research in all its aspects, ensuring an adequate supply of trained scientific manpower for education, industry, agriculture and so on. Even earlier, in 1956, Parliament had adopted an industrial policy resolution which lays down broadly the role of industry and its place in Indian society. There is however no analogous resolution which defines the chief objectives of communications and its function in the Indian democratic set up. An attempt to draw up a communications policy resolution was made in the Ministry of Information and Broadcasting in the early seventies. It was considered that the adoption of such a resolution by Parliament would establish certain basic objectives which would not be subject to alteration from one minister to the next and could therefore be pursued with some consistency over a reasonable period. This exercise was not carried very far; at any rate no such communications policy resolution was ever discussed in Parliament.

An official paper presented to the International Commission for the Study of Communication Problems (the MacBride Commission) on its visit to India in March 1979, drew attention to some of the difficulties in the way of a precisely defined national communications policy in a country which has accepted a mixed economy. This paper has been published in the journal of the Indian Institute of Mass Communication (*The Communicator,* Vol XI No.2, April 1979). The press, cinema and theatre, it points out, are in the private sector; radio and television are under government control. Short films of an informational and educative character are made both by private and government agencies.

While broadcasting and film censorship lie within the exclusive jurisdiction of the central government, information extension services in the rural areas, conducted by what are known as field publicity organisations, are operated by the centre and the state governments.

Broadly speaking, one might say that these difficulties in the way of a national communications policy arose out of the historical situation and have been compounded by responsibilities which the government in a general, but not precisely formulated manner, feels it is called upon to shoulder. The democratic set-up in India would imply for the media freedom from government control. The press and the film industry had developed in the private sector in the British period, radio had not. Consistency would mean that radio and subsequently television should have been placed with the film outside the governmental orbit. We have seen what has happened over the years. From the socialist side of Indian thinking comes the impulse to curtail the power of private capital to control media. Press Commissions appointed by government have been concerned over the manner in which the main newspaper chains in the country are controlled by big business houses. Radical measures to de-link newspapers from business houses have been under consideration for years but no action has been taken. What government has done is to assist and encourage the small newspapers. The setting up of the Film Finance Corporation is a similar attempt to limit the control which film distributors and financiers exercise over the film directors. This approach also explains film censorship because those who generally finance films are interested in making money, not in the making of films, and are ever ready to exploit the medium to achieve their ends. However as one can see these two lines of thinking, the democratic and the socialist, if pushed too far could well lead to situations which they were not intended to create. If there is hesitation and lack of consistency in government policy, one can view it as arising from the apparent conflict of these impulses in a mixed economy.

The same official paper drew attention to the concept of communications in support of development stated in the first Five Year Plan document already mentioned:

A widespread understanding of the Plan is an essential stage in its fulfilment. An understanding of the priorities which govern the

Plan will enable each person to relate his or her role to the larger purposes of the nation as a whole. All available methods of communication have to be developed and the people approached through the written and the spoken word no less than through radio, film, song and drama.

This is a communication policy if you will; whether it has been consistently pursued and developed is a different matter. The Plan outlays on broadcasting cited earlier demonstrate the actual importance assigned to radio and TV.

The following reference in this official paper to the press is relevant, especially since for many people a communication policy in respect of the press is linked with governmental control:

Our Constitution guarantees freedom of speech and expression. Thus the freedom of the press is an act of faith with us. The press has an important role in giving expression to national aspirations. Therefore the government values its freedom and would impose no obligations on it. It is for the press itself to regulate its conduct. The government does not regard the press as a compulsive foe or a bounden ally. In the common tasks of national development the government expects the press to extend its cooperation, even by being critical of it as occasions would demand.

Broadcasting support for development through rural programmes and formal and non-formal education as described in preceding chapters goes back to the earliest beginnings of AIR. In addition to its immediate objectives broadcasting has fostered and kept alive what is best in Indian tradition and culture, such as classical and folk music, and has helped to create a national consciousness by interpreting the culture, drama and literature of each linguistic area to the others. Recognition within the organisation that a monopoly broadcasting system is there to serve society as a whole and not merely the party in power has been a potent factor in the current moves for autonomy.

In an open society initiatives for the formulation of a national policy on communication issues can emanate from a variety of sources. Initiative can come from an important individual. A leading instance in India is the concept of the use of television as a means of education and social change in the villages formulated and publicised by Dr Vikram Sarabhai, which culminated in SITE. Before the decision was made a number of seminars were held in different parts of the country in which scientists, social scientists, broadcasters, communicators, extension workers within government and outsiders participated, so that all aspects of the matter could be exposed and a broad consensus arrived at. Initiative can be taken by government, as in 1973, for example when, a government seminar was organised through AIR on the proper use of television as an instrument for education.

In general the procedure adopted in the past was to raise a public debate on radio and television in the press and through the holding of seminars on all important public issues. The public debate helped to bring into clearer focus the issues involved and give an indication of public sentiment in relation to the various choices before the policy-makers. Since 1980 all this has been forgotten with the government becoming more and more authoritarian. However there are indications of a change, as indicated, for example by Mr Rajiv Gandhi's initiative to raise a public debate on the vexed question of personal law.

It seems improbable, as of now, that the government will formulate a single all-inclusive communications policy for reasons already stated. Sections of the community doubt that such a policy formulation is desirable, and this view has been expressed by no less a person than the chairman of the Press Commission. Important issues are likely to be tackled piecemeal as they arise, in terms of the general constitutional framework and the objectives of the party in power.

The present study of broadcasting within a governmental system was not undertaken with any preconceived hypothesis in mind. Certain broad conclusions emerge from the facts. If the governmental system is centre-based and functions in accordance with standardised procedures it will be against granting procedural (functional) or political autonomy to any of its constituent organisations. We have come up against this problem time and again. Whether it has been in the domain of finance, management structures or political responsibility, the overall system does not recognise exceptions and insists on conformity however much the job to be accomplished demands its own special treatment.

APPENDIX

Television Centres in India: Existing and Proposed
(as on 1 March 1984)

Full-fledged TV Centres

Bangalore
Bombay
Calcutta
Delhi
Hyderabad
Jalandhar
Lucknow
Madras
Srinagar

Proposed TV Centres

Ahmedabad
Bhopal
Bhubaneshwar
Gauhati
Gorakhpur
Nagpur
Patna
Rajkot
Ranchi
Trivandrum

Existing High-Power Transmitters

Ahmedabad
Allahabad
Amritsar
Asansol
Gulbarga
Jaipur
Kanpur
Mussoorie
Muzaffarpur
Nagpur
Panaji
Pij
Pune
Raipur
Sambalpur

Proposed High-Power Transmitters

Agartala
Agra
Bhatinda
Cochin
Cuttack
Dwarka
Indore
Jammu
Kasauli
Kodaikanal
Kurseong
Murshidabad
Poonch
Varanasi
Vijayawada
Visakhapatnam

Existing Low-Power Transmitters

Agartala
Aizawl
Bhopal
Cuttack
Deoriah
Gangtok
Gauhati
Gwalior
Imphal
Indore

Proposed Low-Power Transmitters

Adoni
Ahmadnagar
Ajmer
Aligarh
Alwar
Anantapur
Aurangabad
Balurghat
Barmer
Bellary

Existing Low-Power Transmitters (Contd.)   *Proposed Low-Power Transmitters* (Contd.)

Existing Low-Power Transmitters (Contd.)	Proposed Low-Power Transmitters (Contd.)
Itanagar	Berhampur
Jammu	Bhadravati
Kakinada	Bhagalpur
Kohima	Bharuch
Malda	Bhavnagar
Munger	Bhiwani
Shillong	Bhusawal
Shimla	Bijapur
Suratgarh	Bikaner
Trivandrum	Burhanpur
	Calicut
	Chandrapur
	Coimbatore
	Cuddapah
	Darbhanga
	Devangere
	Dhanbad
	Dharwad
	Dhule
	Dibrugarh
	Etawah
	Faridabad
	Gadagbetkari
	Gaya
	Gondiya
	Hissar
	Jabalpur
	Jaisalmer
	Jalgaon
	Jalna
	Jodhpur
	Kanpur
	Kargil
	Karimnagar
	Korba
	Kulu
	Kumbakonam
	Latur
	Leh
	Loktak
	Malegaon
	Mangalore
	Mehboobnagar
	Murwara
	Mysore
	Nainital
	Nanded
	Nasik

Proposed Low-Power Transmitters (Contd.)

Navasari
Neyveli
Nizamabad
Palghat
Parbhani
Patan
Pauri
Pondicherry
Rae Bareli
Raichur
Rajamundry
Rampur
Rourkela
Sambhal
Sangli
Santiniketan
Shahjahanpur
Sholapur
Siliguri
Sultanpur
Singrauli
Tirupati
Tura
Tiruchirapalli
Vadodara
Udaipur
Vellore
Warangal

Maintenance Bases

Akola
Bardhman
Bareilly
Belgaum
Bilaspur
Cannanore
Bhilwara
Faizabad
Ganganagar
Kurnool
Hospet
Jamshedpur
Pathankot
Purnea
Sagar
Salem
Surat
Tejpur

Source: Ministry or Information and Broadcasting, Report to Parliament, 1983-84, p. 29.

Index